KA-BOOM!

A Dictionary of Comic Book Words,
Symbols & Onomatopoeia

Comprising Many Hundreds of New Words which
Modern Literature, Science & Philosophy have
Neglected to Acknowledge as True, Proper &
Useful Terms & Which Have Never Before Been
Published in Any Lexicon

Compiled & Edited by Kevin J. Taylor

Mora
Publications

Front cover artist: Werner Mueck
http://www.sirbrak.com/

Other works by Kevin Taylor:
Souls Arriving
ISBN 978-0-9732608-3-0
Seize the Stage! A little book on creating poetry
ISBN 978-0-9732608-4-7

Cataloguing in Publication Data

Taylor, Kevin, 1956-
KA-BOOM! A dictionary of comic book words, symbols & onomatopoeia

Includes BZZURKK! The thesaurus of champions / previously published separately in electronic format.

ISBN 978-1-4303-1441-7

1. Comic books, strips, etc.--Dialogue--Dictionaries. 2. Cartoon captions--Dictionaries. 3. Comic books, strips, etc.--Dictionaries.
I. Taylor, Kevin, 1956- . Bzzurkk! II. Title.
PN6707.T39 2006   741.5'03   C2006-905904-7

Published in USA by Lulu.com

© 2007 Kevin J. Taylor. KA-BOOM! A Dictionary of Comic Book Words, Symbols & Onomatopoeia and its companion work BZZURKK! The Thesaurus of Champions are the sole property of Kevin J. Taylor ... taka taka tak ...

Contents

- 7 - Symbols
- 7 - A-Z
- 91 - BZZURKK! The Thesaurus of Champions
- 109 - Appendix A – Base Forms
- 120 - Appendix B – Submissions
- 121 - Appendix C – Reference

Symbols

Editor's note: *The use of symbols to represent words & unspoken concepts, set mood, tone etc is common. Only those symbols most often used or of unusual interest have been included here. Many more can be found.*
! [The Adventures of Tintin: Explorers on the Moon, 1954] An indication of surprise, wonderment etc
$#!* [Pitt #1, 1993] A disguised swear word "Holy $#!*! He's still standing!!"
@$$#*!# [Pitt #1, 1993] A thinly disguised insult word "Have you been an @$$#*!# all your life, or is this a recent development?"
...... [G.I.Joe vol.1 #104, 1990] Signifies waiting
? [The Adventures of Tintin: Explorers on the Moon, 1954] Signifies puzzlement or the condition of not understanding: [MAD #221, March 1981] A symbol indicating wonderment

A-Z

Editor's note: *Comic words beginning in A are usually vocalizations; most often a cry of pain, fear or suffering.*
AAAA [Dare Devil The Man Without Fear vol.1 #3, 1993]:
AAAAA [Avengers West Coast Annual vol.2 #8, 1993]:
AAAAAA [Ragman Cry Of The Dead vol.1 #1, 1993]:
AAAAAAAAA [The Punisher War Zone vol.1 #1, 1993]:
AAAAGGHH [Star Hunters vol.2 #5, 1978]: AAAAGH [Dead Pool: The Circle Chase vol.1 #4, 1993]: AAAAARGH [2099 Unlimited vol.1 #3, 1993]: AAAAGGH [Mantra: Infinity 1995]: AAAARRRRGH [G.I.Joe vol.1 #104, 1990]: AAAARRRGHHH [2099 Unlimited vol.1 #3, 1993]: AAAARRRRR [Avengers West Coast Annual vol.2 #8, 1993]: AAAG [Dare Devil The Man Without Fear vol.1 #2, 1993]: AAAGG [Dare Devil The Man Without Fear vol.1 #3, 1993]: AAAGGGH [Star Hunters vol.2 #5, 1978]: AAAGGGK also AAAGGK [Avengers West Coast Annual vol.2 #8, 1993]: AAAHH [The Adventures Of Tintin: Explorers On The Moon, 1954]: AAAHHRR [2099 Unlimited vol.1 #2, 1993]: AAAIIEEE [Catwoman #6, 1994]: AAAK also AAAAK [Cold Blooded Chamelion Commando #1, 1986]: AAAKHH [Fantastic Four #315]: AAARGHHH [Rune #1, 1994]: AARGH [Prototype vol.1 #1, 1994]: AARRH [2099 Unlimited vol.1 #3,

1993]: AARRHH [Pitt #1, 1993] AARRGGGGG also
AARRRRR [Avengers West Coast Annual vol.2 #8, 1993]:
AGHHHHHHH [Venom The Enemy Within vol.1 #1, 1994]:
AGHA [Venom The Enemy Within vol.1 #2, 1994]: AGHH
also AGHHH also AGHHHHHH [Venom The Enemy Within
vol.1 #1, 1994]: AGH-K [Batman #502, 1993]: AHH [Man Of
War #8]: AIEGHH also AKKKK [X-Factor vol.1 #84, 1992]:
AOWW [Clint: The Hamster Triumphant #1, 1986]: ARGGH
[Cable #5, 1993]: ARRGHH also ARRGHHH [ROM #43,
1983]: ARRHH [X-Factor vol.1 #84, 1992]: ARRRGHHH [The
Vision and The Scarlet Witch vol.2 #7, 1986]: ARRRRRR
[Avengers West Coast Annual vol.2 #8, 1993]: A cry of pain:
AAAAAAA--* [NFL SuperPro vol.1 #9, 1992] A final cry of
pain, suffering etc: AGK [Darkhold: Pages From The Book Of
Sins vol.1 #7, 1993] A final utterance of pain
AAAAA [Dakota North vol.1 #3, 1986] A cry made by
someone falling
AAAAAA also **AAAAAAA** [NFL SuperPro vol.1 #9, 1992] A
cry of fear
AAAAAA see AAAA
AAAAAAA see AAAAAA
AAAAAAA--* see AAAA
AAAAAAAAAA see AAAA
AAAAAAAGHHHH [Dead Pool The Circle Chase #4, 1993]
A cry of horror
AAAAAAAHHHHHHH [Pitt #1, 1993] A cry of terror
AAAAAARGH see AAAA
AAAAGGH see AAAA
AAAAGGHH see AAAA
AAAAGH see AAAA
AAAAGHH [MAD #227, December 1981] A cry of suffering
AAAAHH see AAAA
AAAAK see AAAA
AAAARGH [MAD #244, January 1984] A cry of surprise
AAAARRRGHHH see AAAA
AAAARRRRGH see AAAA
AAAARRRRR see AAAA
A-A-ACHOO [Kool Asthma Kids #2, 1996] The sound of a
sneeze
AAAG see AAAA
AAAGG see AAAA
AAAGGGH see AAAA
AAAGGGK see AAAA
AAAGGK see AAAA
AAAHH [Mantra vol.1 #5, 1993] A cry of fear

AAAHHHRR see AAAA
AAAIIEEE see AAAA
AAAK see AAAA
AAAKHH see AAAA
AAARGH also AAAARGH [The Anomalies #1, 2000] An utterance of protest or dismay
AAARGHHH see AAAA
AACHOOOOO [The Ren and Stimpy Show #6, 1993] The sound of a sneeze
AAEEEK [MAD #222, April 1981] A cry of fear
AAHH [MAD #177, September 1975] An exclamation of admiration
AAH-OOOH-GAH [Iron Man #277, 1992] A hornlike sound signifying the end of the world
AAIIEEEE also AAIIIEEEEE [Darkhold #10, 1993] A martial arts cry
AAIIIEEEEE see AAIIEEEE
AARRGH [X-Factor vol.1 #8, 1992] A growling sound
AARRH see AAAA
AARRHH see AAAA
AARRRGGGGG see AAAA
AARRRRR see AAAA
ABSOLUTE-A-MENTE [Betty #40] Absolutely, without a doubt
ACK-YAK [MAD's Don Martin Cooks Up More Tales, 1976] The struggling sounds of a dying man
AEEEE [Mantra vol.1 #7, 1994] A cry of pain
AGGGH [Mantra vol.1 #2, 1993] A cry of pain
AGGH [MAD #227, December 1981] A sound made while grasping one's throat and pretending to die
AGGHHHHHHH see AAAA
AGH [MAD #202, December 1978] A grunting sound
AGHA see AAAA
AGHH see AAAA
AGHHH see AAAA
AGHHHHHH see AAAA
AGH-K see AAAA
AGK [Darkhold: Pages From The Book Of Sins vol.1 #7, 1993] A final utterance of pain
AGOOOOOGAH [Mantra vol.1 #5, 1993] A cry similar to that of a horn type alarm, as on a submarine, indicating excitement, pleasure etc
AH [The Adventures of Captain Jack #7, 1987] A sound of enjoyment: [The Adventures of Bayou Billy #2, 1989] An exclamation of realization or discovery

AHEM [Star Hunters vol.2 #4, 1978] A sound made when clearing the throat: AH-HEM [Betty #40] The sound made when clearing the throat, especially to express displeasure or disapproval with, or to get the attention of, another
AHA [G.I.Joe vol.1 #60, 1987] An exclamation of discovery
AHH see AAAA
AH-HAH [MAD #249, September 1984] An exclamation of discovery
AH-HEM see AHEM
AHHH [G.I.Joe vol.1 #60, 1987] An utterance expressing satisfaction, pleasure, etc: [Pitt #1, 1993] A cry of terror: also AHHHHHHHH [Cold Blooded Chamelion Commando #1, 1986] A cry of sudden fear
AHHHHHGH [Ragman Cry Of The Dead #1] A scream
AHHHHHH [MAD #214, April 1980] A prolonged sound indicating relief
AHHHHHHHH see AHHH
AIEE [Clint: The Hamster Triumphant #1, 1986] The cry of someone falling, as out of a helicopter
AIEGHH see AAAA
AIIEEE also AIIIIE [Ripley's Believe It Or Not: True Ghost Stories #53, 1975] A cry of anguish, fear, pain etc
AIIIIE see AIIEEE
AKKK [The Solution #5] A startled cry
AKKKK see AAAA
AOOG also AOOGAOOGAOO [G.I.Joe #61, 1987]: AROOGA [The Anomalies #1, 2000]: AROOGAH also AROOGAHAROOGAH [Darkhold #10, 1993] The sound of a horn type alarm
AOOGAOOGAOO see AOOG
ARF also ARFF also A-RUFF [Superboy #154, 1969] The sound of a dog's bark
ARFF see ARF
ARG [MAD #202, December 1978] A grunting sound
ARGGH see AAAA
ARGH [MAD #175, June 1975] The sound made by a dying person: [MAD #222, April 1981] A muffled cry of fear
AROGAH see AOOG
AROOGA see AOOG
AROOGAHAROOGAH see AOOG
AROOOO [Dare Devil #194] The sound of baying
ARRARGH [MAD #211, December 1979] A fighting cry: [MAD #221, March 1981] A sound made during lovemaking: [MAD #221, March 1981] A sound made to frighten others
ARRARGLE [MAD #221, March 1981] A throat sound

ARRGH [MAD #221, March 1981] The sound of a normal sized body morphing to a larger one
Arrrgh [MAD #225, September 1981] A growling sound signifying anger
ARRGHH see AAAA
ARRGHHH see AAAA
ARRHH see AAAA
ARRRGH [2099 Unlimited vol.1 #4, 1993] A cry of anguish
ARRRRGH [New Kids On The Block: Magic Summer Tour, 1990] A cry made to frighten another
ARRRRRGH [MAD #218, October 1980] The occasional sound of the Pink Panther
ARRRRROOOOO [Hawkeye vol.2 #2, 1994] A baying sound
ARRRRRR see AAAA
A-RUFF see ARF
AWK [MAD #175, June 1975] A sound made by a dying person
AWROOOO [ROM #37, 1982] A haunting, ghostly sound
AWWW [Cold Blooded Chamelion Commando #1, 1986] A prolonged "ah" sound
BAAA-DOOOW [Ultraman vol.1 #2, 1994] The sound of an explosion
BAAA-ROOMM see BAA-ROOM
BAA-ROOM also BAAA-ROOMM [Ultraman vol.1 #1, 1994] also BAAAROOOOM [Ultraman vol.1 #2, 1994] The sound of an explosion
BAAAROOOOM see BAA-ROOM
BAAARRRRFFFF [MAD #241, September 1983] The sound of vomiting
BA-BAMM [The Adventures of Bayou Billy #4, 1990] The sound of a collision
BADOOM see BA-DOOOMM
BA-DOOOMM [Captain Atom #7] also BADOOM [2099 Unlimited vol.1 #4, 1993] The sound of an explosion
BADABOOM [War vol.1 #1, 1994] The sound of an explosion
BAH [Bobby Sherman #6, 1972] An exclamation of surprise: [Captain Marvel vol.1 #42, 1976] An exclamation of disdain
BAHWAHHHH [The Adventures of Bayou Billy #4, 1990] The sound of a vehicle downshifting
BALLOOM [MAD's Don Martin Cooks Up More Tales, 1976] The sound of a volcano beginning to erupt
BAM [Attack #41, 1983] The sound of a gunshot; The sound of an explosion: [Prototype vol.1 #6, 1994] The sound of a door being kicked in: [MAD #218, October 1980] A sound made by pounding on a door: [The Ren and Stimpy Show #6,

1993] The sound made by a punch: [MAD #224, January 1981] The sound of a plant pot to the head: [Emiril Live, TV] The sound of kicking it up a notch: BAMM [Captain Atom #7] The sound of a gunshot

BAMF [X-Men] The sound of Nightcrawler teleporting himself, as in air rushing to fill the void where he instantly was.

BAMM see BAM

BANG [The Adventures Of Tintin: Explorers On The Moon, 1954] The sound of a gunshot: [Madballs vol.1 #7, 1987] A mechanical sound caused by a sudden impact: [MAD #212, January 1980] A word used by children to simulate gunfire: [MAD #218, October 1980] The sound made by a tire going flat: [MAD #241, September 1983] The sound of hard knocking on a door

BANG CRASH [MAD #222, April 1981] The sound of drums

BANG CRASH BOOM [Archie #407, 1993] A sound describing the loud sounds of rock music

BAOOOM [The Twisted Tantrum of the Purple Snit #1, 1980] The sound of bazooka fire

BAOUM [Batman #502, 1993] The sound of weapon fire

BAP [G.I.Joe vol.1 #61, 1987] The sound of an object being struck

Bap-de-bow... [MAD's Don Martin Cooks Up More Tales, 1976] Musical instrument sounds

BAPP [The Adventures of Bayou Billy #4, 1990] A punching sound; A kicking sound

BARF... [MAD #212, January 1980] A vomiting sound: also BARF [MAD #222, April 1981]

BAROOM [MAD #244, January 1984] The sound of an explosion

BA-R-RA-ROOM [The Adventures of Bob Hope #95, 1965] The exploding sound of a failed experiment

BARROOM also BARROOOM [Ultraman vol.1 #2, 1994] The sound of an explosion

BA-RROO-MM [New Kids On The Block: Magic Summer Tour, 1990] The roaring sound of a motorcycle

BARROOOM see BARROOM

BASH [Madballs vol.1 #7, 1987] The sound of a collision

BATANG [The Twisted Tantrum of the Purple Snit #1, 1980] A sound of people and equipment in operation, as might be heard on a construction site

BA-TANG [Thunderstrike vol.1 #2, 1994] The banging sound of a mace hitting an object

BAWWWW [The Adventures of Captain Jack #7, 1987] The sound of crying

BAZAKK [Thunderstrike vol.1 #4, 1994] The crackling, electrical sound of an energy beam

BBBARRROOOMM [Crackbusters #1, 1986] The sound of an explosion

BBBDROOM [Ralph Snart Adventures vol.5, 1993] The sound of a car motor

BBZZTTT also BBZZZTT [Crackbusters #1, 1986] The sound of a buzzing intercom

BBZZZTT see BBZZTTT

BDAM [Batman #502, 1993] The sound of a gunshot

B-DAMM-D-D [New Kids On The Block: Magic Summer Tour, 1990] The sound of thunder

BDOK [Captain Marvel vol.1 #42, 1976] The sound of a kick to the head

BDOW [Captain Marvel vol.1 #42, 1976] A hitting sound

BEEP [The Adventures Of Tintin: Explorers On The Moon, 1954] The sound of a radar signal: [The Punisher: War Zone vol.1 #1, 1993] The sound of a telephone answering device message indicator: [Man of War #8] The sound of an intercom alert: [Ripley's Believe It Or Not: True Ghost Stories #53, 1975] The sound of a roadrunner: [MAD #246, April 1984] also BEEEEP also BEEEEEP [Dare Devil #277] The sound of a vehicle horn: also BEEEEEEEP [MAD #246, April 1984] The sound of an extended electronic indicator

BEEEEP see BEEP

BEEEEEP see BEEP

BEEEEEEEP see BEEP

BEOW [Attack #41, 1983] The sound of a bullet in flight

BEEYOOP [MAD #221, March 1981] The sound of a large body morphing into a smaller sized one

BELLLCCH [MAD #218, October 1980] A belching sound

BHWOOOM [Batman #502, 1993] The sound of an explosion

BIFF [The Adventures of Bayou Billy #3, 1990] A hitting sound

BING [MAD #219, December 1980] The sound of a fire station alarm bell

BING BONG [MAD #231, June 1982] The sound of a doorbell

BLA also BLABBLA [MAD #241, September 1983] The sound of someone talking

BLABBLA see BLA

BLACCH [MAD #249, September 1984] The sound of vomiting

BLA-DRAMM [The Adventures of Bayou Billy #4, 1990] The sound of a shotgun blast

BLA-DROOOM [The Adventures of Bayou Billy #4, 1990] The sound of an explosion

BLAH-DA BOOOOOM [The Adventures of Bayou Billy #4, 1990] The sound of an explosion

BLAM [Our Fighting Forces #111, 1968] The sound of a tank cannon; The sound of mortar fire: [MAD #178, October 1975] The sound of a gunshot: [MAD #214, April 1980] The sound of a bomb: [MAD #252, January 1985] The sound of a collision: [The Ren and Stimpy Show vol.1 #6, 1993] A hitting sound: [Fightin' Marines #145, 1979]: [MAD #177, September 1975] also BLA-AAAAM [War Machine vol.1 #1, 1994] also BLAAM [Our Fighting Forces #111, 1968]: The sound of an explosion: also BLAAMMM [G.I.Joe vol.1 #104, 1990] also BLAMM [Avengers West Coast Annual vol.2 #8, 1993] The sound of gunfire: [Attack #41, 1983]: BLAM BLAM [MAD Super Special 16, 1975] also BLAMBLAM [Avengers West Coast Annual vol.2 #8, 1993] The sound of multiple gunshots: also BLAMM [MAD #241, September 1983] The sound of a gunshot

BLA-AAAAM see BLAM

BLAAM see BLAM

BLAAMMM see BLAM

BLAMBLAM see BLAM

BLAMM see BLAM

BLAMP [MAD #216, July 1980] The sound of a bullet biting into wood: [MAD #221, March 1981] A sound made during lovemaking

BLANG [The Ren and Stimpy Show vol.1 #6, 1993] The sound of a pipe hitting a head

BLAP [MAD #211, December 1979] The sound of food being splashed: [Cold Blooded Chamelion Commando #1, 1986] The sound of a shell casing being ejected from an automatic weapon; The peculiar sound of a chamelion tongue achieving its target

BLASHH [Batman #502, 1993] The sound of plate glass breaking

BLAST [MAD #218, October 1980] The sound of an explosion

BLAT [Ralph Snart Adventures vol.5, 1993] The sound of someone being slammed to the floor

BLAT BLAT [MAD #241, September 1983] The sound of a truck's air horn

BLATCH [MAD #211, December 1979] An eating sound

BLBBL FLB BLBBPLP [Knights of Pendragon #13] The sound of bubbles made by a drowning person
BLEAH [The Anomalies #1, 2000] An utterance expressing distaste
BLECCH [MAD #212, January 1980] The sound of a monster consuming a person
BLEEP [MAD #224, January 1981] The sound of breasts suddenly enlarging
BLESHH [Batman #502, 1993] The sound of weapon fire hitting a (presumably soft) target
BLEUGHZ [Ralph Snart Adventures vol.5, 1993] The sound made by cutting into a rapidly decaying body
BLIF [MAD #211, December 1979] The sound of food being flung from a fork
BLIKX [Ralph Snart Adventures vol.5, 1993] The sound made by a punch in the nose
BLINK [MAD's Don Martin Cooks Up More Tales, 1976] The gentle sound of a blink
BLINK-DIT [MAD's Don Martin Cooks Up More Tales, 1976] The sound of a contact lens popping out
BLIP [MAD #215, June 1980] A censorship sound, usually editing out a swear word
BLOIT [MAD #224, January 1981] The sound of a muscle popping
BLONK [The Ren and Stimpy Show vol.1 #6, 1993] The sound of an object being knocked over
BLOOSH [2099 Unlimited vol.1 #3, 1993] The sound of an explosion in water
BLOP [MAD #233, September 1982] The sound soup makes
BLORP [The Ren and Stimpy Show vol.1 #6, 1993] The slopping sound of a liquid
BLORSH [2099 Unlimited vol.1 #3, 1993] A splashing sound
BLUB [The Adventures of Bayou Billy #4, 1990] Bubble sounds as those made when a head is held under water
BLUNNT [Knights of Pendragon #13] A sound made by kicking something
BMPH [Ultraman vol.1 #1, 1994] The sound a person makes when they fall and hit the floor
BOAM also **BOAMM** [Batman #502, 1993] The sound of weapon fire
BOAMM see BOAM
BOIING [MAD #225, September 1981] The sound of a shirt collar popping out of a suit jacket
BOING SMACK [MAD #229, March 1982] The sound of a bell-ringer kiss
BOINK [Dare Devil #194] The sound of a ball bouncing

BOK [Captain Marvel vol.1 #42, 1976] also BOKK [Batman #502, 1993] A hitting sound
BOKK see BOK
BOM [MAD #227, December 1981] The sound of a dance beat
BONG [MAD #219, December 1980] The sound of an elevator floor indicator bell: [MAD #252, January 1985] The sound of a needle on a weigh scale reaching its limit: also BONNG [MAD #188, January 1977] The sound of a bell
BONNG see BONG
BONK [G.I.Joe vol.1 #60, 1987] The sound made by one vehicle striking a glancing blow to another: [Clint: The Hamster Triumphant #1, 1986] The sound made by an object striking the head
BOOM [MAD #177, September 1975] The sound of a bolt of lightning: [MAD's Don Martin Cooks Up More Tales, 1976] The sound of a volcano beginning to erupt: [MAD #218, October 1980] A sound made by pounding on a door: [MAD #222, April 1981] The sound of a bass drum: [Madballs vol.1 #7, 1987] The sound of an object hitting the ground; The sound of a sonic blast: [G.I.Joe vol.1 #60, 1987] The sound of a large explosion: [The Punisher: War Zone vol.1 #1, 1993] The sound of a shotgun blast: The sound of a gunshot: [Ralph Snart Adventures vol.5, 1993] The sound of an explosion: The sound of cannon fire: [FREEX #7, 1994] The sound of bullets ricocheting off an object: [The Adventures of Kool-Aid Man #6, 1989] The sound of a footstep: BOOM-KA-BOOM [Captain Atom #7] The sound of multiple explosions: BOOMM [Fightin' Marines #145, 1979] also BOOOM [X-Factor vol.1 #84, 1992] also BOOOMM [Captain Atom #7] also BOOOOM [MAD #212, January 1980] also BOOOOOM [War Machine vol.1 #1, 1994] The sound of an explosion: [The Twisted Tantrum of the Purple Snit #1, 1980] A sound of people and equipment in operation, as might be heard on a construction site
BOOM-KA-BOOM see BOOM
BOOMER-ROOM [MAD #238, April 1983] The sound of a laxative suddenly taking effect
BOOMM see BOOM
BOOOM see BOOM
BOOOMM see BOOM
BOOOOM see BOOM
BOOOOOM see BOOMBOOP [The Adventures of Bayou Billy #4, 1990] A bubble sound as made when a head is held under water

BOP [Madballs vol.1 #1, 1987] The sound made by objects colliding in mid air: [2099 Unlimited vol.1 #3, 1993] A hitting sound

BOSH [MAD #217, September 1980] The sound of a bottle of champagne breaking during the launching ceremony of a boat

BRAAAAM [Pitt #1, 1993] The sound of an explosion

BRAAAAOWN [Pitt #1, 1993] The sound of a motorcycle engine

BRAAAP see BRAP

BRAAP see BRAP

BRACK [2099 Unlimited vol.1 #3, 1993] A hitting sound

BRAK [Dakota North vol.1 #3, 1986] The sound of a gunshot; A kicking sound

BRAKA [Dare Devil The Man Without Fear vol.1 #3, 1993] also BRAKABRAKABRAKA [Dare Devil The Man Without Fear vol.1 #5, 1994] The sound of automatic gunfire

BRAKABRAKABRAKA see BRAKA

BRAKK [The Vision and The Scarlet Witch vol.2 #7, 1986] A punching sound: [The Adventures of Bayou Billy #4, 1990] also BRAK-K [The Adventures of Bayou Billy #3, 1989] The sound of a door being smashed down

BRA-KOOOM [Darkhold #10, 1993] The sound of an explosion

BRAKT [2099 Unlimited vol.1 #2, 1993] A kicking sound

BRAM [Steel #1.1994] The sound of a collision

BRAP [Our Fighting Forces #111, 1968] also BRAAP [Our Fighting Forces #111, 1968] The sound made firing an M-16 machine gun: [The Punisher: War Zone vol.1 #1, 1993] also BRAAAP; The sound made by firing off a thirty round clip of nine mils

BRATATAT [Darkhold 10, 1993] also BRAT A TAT A TAT [Darkhold: Pages from the Book of Sins vol.1 #7, 1993] also BRAT-A-TAT-TAT [The Adventures of Bayou Billy #2, 1989] The sound of machine gun fire

BRAT A TAT A TAT see BRATATAT

BRAT-A-TAT-TAT see BRATATAT

BRATCH [Batman #502, 1993] The sound of weapon fire hitting an object

BRAX [Ralph Snart Adventures vol.5, 1993] A belching sound

BRDAP [MAD #227, December 1981] A sound from a pinball machine

BREEESH [Batman #502, 1993] The sound of breaking glass

BREENG [MAD's Don Martin Cooks Up More Tales, 1976] The sound of a telephone ringing

BREEP [The Solution vol.5] The sound by an electronic warning indicator of a security breach

BRIIIIIIING see BRINGG

BRINGG [Mantra vol.1 #5, 1993] also **BRIIIIIING** [Batman #502, 1993] also **BRINNG** [Mantra: Infinity, 1995] The sound of a telephone ringing

BRINNG see BRINGG

BRIT also **BRITT** [The Adventures of Bayou Billy #4, 1990] The sound of a bullet hitting the ground

BRITT see BRIT

BRMMMMMMMMMMMMMMMMMMMMM [The Adventures of Captain Jack #7, 1987] The sound of a drum roll

BRNNGT [MAD #231, June 1982] The sound of a telephone ring tone

BROK [NFL SuperPro vol.1 #9, 1992] A hitting sound: [Steel #1.1994] A punching sound

BROUM also **BROUMMM** also **BRROUUMM** [Lucky Luke Canyon Apache, 1971] The sound of a boulder falling

BROUMMM see BROUM

BRROUUMM see BROUM

BRRA-A-A-AP [Our Fighting Forces #111, 1968] The sound of an M-16 machine gun

BRRAAOOOM [Pitt #1, 1993] The sound of a motorcycle engine

BRRRAP also **BRRRAPP** [G.I.Joe vol.1 #104, 1990] also **BRRRAAAP** [G.I.Joe vol.1 #104, 1990] The sound of machine gun fire

BRRRAAAP see BRRRAP

BRRRAPP see BRRRAP

BRRRR also **BRRRRP** [Our Fighting Forces #111, 1968] The sound of machine gun fire

BRRRRP see BRRRR

BrrrT [Mantra vol.1 #2, 1993] also **BRRRRRRT** also **BRRRTTT** [Mantra vol.1 #7, 1994] The sound of automatic weapon fire

BRRRRRRT see BrrrT

BRRRTTT see BrrrT

BRRZZT [Star Hunters vol.2 #4, 1978] The sound of electronic weapon fire

BRRRZZZZZZAP [MAD #230, April 1982] The sound of an electric chair execution

BTAM [The Solution #5] A hitting sound

BTHWAKKT [Thunderstrike vol.1 #4, 1994] A hitting sound made a door being smashed open

BTOK [Avengers West Coast Annual vol.2 #8, 1993] A hitting sound

BTOOOM [Avengers West Coast Annual vol.2 #8, 1993] The sound of an explosion

BUDA also **BUDDA** also **BUDDABUDDA** [Our Fighting Forces #111, 1968] also **BUDDAB** [War Machine vol.1 #1, 1994] The sound of machine gun fire

BUDDA see BUDA

BUDDAB see BUDA

BUDDABUDDA see BUDA

BUDDURP [Attack vol.1, 1983] The sound of machine gun fire

BUDOOOM [The Sandman #55, 1993] The sound of an explosion

BUH-BA-BA-BA-BUHM [Ragman: Cry of the Dead #1] The sound of a drum

BUHBOOM [The Punisher: War Zone vol.1 #1, 1993] The sound made by a 50 caliber nitro express round

BUH-BOOM [Hawkeye vol.2 #3, 1994] The sound of an explosion

**BULL#$%¢&*!** [MAD Super Special 16, 1975] A word similar in meaning and construction to BULL$#!+ [see Symbols]

BUMP [New Kids On The Block: Magic Summer Tour, 1990] The sound of colliding bodies

BURP [MAD #229, March 1982] also **BURPXK** [Ralph Snart Adventures vol.5, 1993] A belching sound

BURPXK see BURP

BURR [The Adventures of Kool-Aid Man #6, 1989] A sound made to indicate coldness or shivering

BUZZ [MAD #241, September 1983] The sound of an alarm

BUZZZ [MAD #229, March 1982] The sound of a buzzer

BWA-HA-HA-HA [The Solution #5] The sound of laughter

BWAK [Venom Lethal Protector #3, 1993] The sound of a punch

BWAKT [Batman #502, 1993] The sound of a door being knocked open

BWAM [Steel #1.1994] A hitting sound

BWEACH [Mantra vol.1 #5, 1993] Means "Breech", as in the idiom "Into the breech"

BWEEE [G.I.Joe vol.1 #61, 1987] The sound of a bullet passing close by

BWOOM also **BWOOOOM** [2099 Unlimited vol.1 #2, 1993] also **BWOOOOOM** [Wonderman #12, 1992] The sound of an

explosion; The sound of a shotgun blast: [2099 Unlimited vol.1 #4, 1993] A hitting sound
BWOOOOM see BWOOM
BWOOOOOM see BWOOM
BWOP [Captain Marvel vol.1 #42, 1976] A hitting sound
BWUMPT [Batman #502, 1993] A sound made by slamming a door into a head
BZZAPP [The Anomalies #1, 2000] A sound of electronic weapon fire
BZZARR also BZZOOORRRR also BZZZZZTT [MAD #227, December 1981] The sound of a chainsaw
BZZOOORRRR see BZZARR
BZZT [Mantra vol.1 #5, 1993] The sound of a buzzer
BZZZ [Dakota North vol.1 #3, 1986] The sound of a telephone buzzer: [Cold Blooded Chamelion Commando #1, 1986] The buzzing sound of a fly: [Darkhold #10, 1993] A buzzing sound
BZZZZ [MAD #230, April 1982] A video buzzing sound
BZZZZZ [MAD's Don Martin Cooks Up More Tales, 1976] The sound of a flying insect
BZZZZZZ [Crackbusters #1, 1986] The sound of an intercom buzzer
BZZZZZZZZZZZZZZZZZCRACK [Warlock vol.2 #3, 1992] The sound of an alarm
BZZZZZTT see BZZARR
CAR-RAM [The Mighty Thor vol.1 #446, 1992] The sound made by an object crashing through a barrier
CAWEE [Clint: The Hamster Triumphant #1, 1986] A bird's cry
CHA-BAMM [2099 Unlimited vol.1 #4, 1993] A hitting sound made by slamming a body into a wall
CHA-CHUNK [2099 Unlimited vol.1 #2, 1993] The sound made by the pump action on a shotgun
CHAK [Dead Pool: The Circle Chase #4, 1993] A mechanical sound made by parts coming undone: [Cable, 1993] The sound of a blade hitting a wall: [Crackbusters #1, 1986] A punching sound
CHAK-A-CHAK-AKK-CHK CHK-CHK see CHAKK-CHAKK-CHAK-CHAK
CHAKKA [2099 Unlimited vol.1 #3, 1993] The sound of machine gun fire
CHAKK-CHAKK-CHAK-CHAK also CHAK-A-CHAK-AKK-CHK CHK-CHK [New Kids On The Block: Magic Summer Tour, 1990] The sound made by helicopter rotors
CHAKT [Batman #502, 1993] The sound of a grenade being released

CHAM [Pitt #1, 1993] A sound of gunfire
CHA-POW POW [The Adventures of Bayou Billy #2, 1989] The sound of multiple gunshots
CHASH [Wonderman #12, 1992] A crashing sound
CHAT-CHOOM [Pitt #1, 1993] The sounds made by the rapid pump action and firing of a shotgun
CHCHASH [Star Hunters vol.2 #5, 1978] The sound of an electronic weapon
CHEWWA also **CHEEEEYEW** also **CHEEEEEYEW** [The Ren and Stimpy Show vol.1 #6, 1993] A chewing sound
CHEEEEYEW see CHEWWA
CHEEEEEYEW see CHEWWA
CHFF [Batman #502, 1993] The sound of a projectile being launched
CHIK [Dead Pool: The Circle Chase #4, 1993] also CHIKKT, A sound made by mechanical parts coming undone: [War Machine vol.1, #1, 1994] A mechanical sound made while fastening parts together, as armor
CHIKKT see CHIK
CHING also **CHINGG** also **CHINKCHKCHAKK** [Dare Devil: The Man Without Fear vol.1 #3, 1993] The sound of chain rattling: also Chinkcnk Chakk [KA-BOOM! 2006] The sound of a loose chain on a chainsaw
CHINGG see CHING
CHINK [2099 Unlimited vol.1 #2, 1993] A sound made when a cup falls and hits the floor
CHINKCHKCHAKK see CHING
Chinkcnk Chakk see CHING
CHIP [MAD #178, October 1975] The sound of an axe shaping wood
CHOK [G.I.Joe vol.1 #104, 1990] The sound of a bullet hitting wood: [Avengers West Coast Annual vol.2 #8, 1993] A sound made by a falling tree: [2099 Unlimited vol.1 #2, 1993] A hitting sound, as of a thrown shoe hitting a face: [Wonderman #12, 1992] A punching sound
CHOKE [MAD #229, March 1982] An accompanying sound to hysterical laughter
CHOMP [Clint #1, 1986] A biting sound: [The Ren and Stimpy Show vol.1 #6, 1993] A sound made while eating: [Venom: The Enemy Within vol.1 #1, 1994] A hitting sound
CHOMPLE [MAD #233, September 1982] An eating sound
CHONK [Steel #1, 1994] The sound of a thrown cast iron frying pan being caught by the handle
CHOOM also **CHOOMSKH** [The Punisher: War Zone vol.1 #1, 1993] The sound of a blast from a sawed-off shotgun:

[2099 Unlimited vol.1 #4, 1993] The sound of an explosion: [Marvel Comics Presents vol.1 #11, 1993] The sound of an inter-dimensional portal opening: [Prototype vol.1 #6, 1994] A sound from an electronic weapon

CHOOMSKH see CHOOM

CHOONT [Venom: Lethal Protector #3, 1993] The sound of a missile launching

CHOP [MAD #178, October 1975] The sound of an axe chopping wood: [The Ren and Stimpy Show vol.1 #6, 1993] A punching sound

CHOW [Pitt #1, 1993] The sound of gunfire

CHPOW [2099 Unlimited vol.1 #2, 1993] The sound of gunfire

CHRAKK [2099 Unlimited vol.1 #3, 1993] A cracking sound

CHTTHZZ [Dead Pool: The Circle Chase #4, 1993] The sound of mechanical parts coming undone

CHUCKLE [MAD's Don Martin Cooks Up More Tales, 1976] The sound of quiet laughter

CHUD [Detective Comics vol.47 #529, 1983] A kicking sound

CHUDD [The Solution vol.1 #2, 1993] A punching sound

CHUFF [Batman #502, 1993] The sound of weapon fire

CHUGGA CHUG CHUG CHUG [MAD #216, July 1980] The sound of a boat engine

CHUK [Dead Pool: The Circle Chase #4, 1993] A punching sound: [Dare Devil: The Man Without Fear vol.1 #4, 1994] The sound made by an elbow connecting with a jaw: [Dare Devil: The Man Without Fear vol.1 #5, 1994] A sound made with a karate chop to the throat

CHUKK [Dare Devil: The Man Without Fear vol.1 #3, 1993] A mechanical sound of chain links knocking together

CHUNK [MAD's Don Martin Cooks Up More Tales, 1976] The sound of a stick thrust into the sand

CLACK [War Machine vol.1 #1, 1994] A mechanical sound made while fastening objects together, as armor

CLACKITY CLACK [MAD #212, January 1980] The sound made by a low rider tricycle

CLANG [Son of MAD, 1973] The sound of a jail cell door slamming shut: [MAD #212, January 1980] The sound of a burglar alarm [The Twisted Tantrum of the Purple Snit #1, 1980] A sound of people and equipment in operation, as might be heard on a construction site: [Madballs vol.1 #7, 1987] A metallic or mechanical sound

CLANK [Our Fighting Forces #111, 1968] A metallic or mechanical banging sound

CLAP [The Night Man vol.1 #4, 1994] The sound of hands clapping together
CLAP CLAP [MAD #214, April 1980] The sound of applause
CLICK [MAD #218, October 1980] The sound made by pressing a button on a TV remote: [MAD #232, July 1982] The sound of a trigger being pulled: [MAD #244, January 1984] The sound of a window being jimmied: [Detective Comics vol.47 #529, 1983] The sound made by a switch: [G.I.Joe vol.1 #104, 1990] The sound made by an Uzi with an empty clip: [Ralph Snart Adventures vol.5, 1993] The sound of a key turning in an ignition switch: also CLIKK [Avengers West Coast Annual vol.2 #8, 1993] A mechanical sound of objects coming into forced contact
CLIKK see CLIK
CLINK [Ripley's Believe It Or Not: True Ghost Stories #53, 1975] The sound of a gold coin falling to the floor
CLIP [MAD #178, October 1975] The sound of shears clipping grass
CLONG [Son of MAD, 1973] The sound of a pipe hit on the head
CLONK [Son of MAD, 1973] The sound of a mallet hitting the ground: [MAD #217, September 1980] The sound of a body being hit by a car: [Clint #1, 1986] A kicking sound
CLOP [Son of MAD, 1973] The sound of a small stone from a sling shot hitting someone in the head: [The Ren and Stimpy Show vol.1 #6, 1993] A kicking sound: also CLOPS [Lucky Luke: Canyon Apache, 1971] A punching sound
CLOPS see CLOP
CLUNK [The Adventures of Bayou Billy #4, 1990] The sound made by a dropped object
CONK [MAD #252, January 1985] The sound of a bottle hitting a head
COOM [The Twisted Tantrum of the Purple Snit #1, 1980] A sound of people and equipment in operation, as might be heard on a construction site
CRAACK see CRACK
CRAAKK see CRACK
CRAASH see CRASH
CRACK [MAD #229, March 1982] The sound of a ski pole breaking: [Our Fighting Forces #111, 1968] A cracking sound; A sound of breaking glass: [Man of War #8] A sound made when a punch or kick connects: also CRAACK [Fightin' Marines #145, 1979] The sound of an artillery shell hitting a tank: [Mantra: Infinity, 1995] A hitting sound: also CRAAKK [Mantra: Infinity, 1995] A hitting sound

CRA....KWOOOM [Thunderstrike vol.1 #4, 1994] The sound of an energy blast
CRANK [The Anomalies #1, 2000] The sound made by a mechanical wall moving: The sound made by pulling a large switch
CRASH [Our Fighting Forces #111, 1968] A crashing sound, as of a collision: [MAD #181, March 1976] The sound of a bottle breaking: [MAD #188, January 1977] The sound of a fist crashing through a wall: [The Incredible Hulk vol.1 #226, 1978] The sound of a ball and chain smashing a wall: [MAD #225, September 1981] The sound of breaking glass: [G.I. Joe vol.1 #60, 1987] The sound made by a door being kicked in: [The Adventures of Kool-Aid Man #6, 1989] A crashing sound: also CRAASH [Venom: The Enemy Within #2, 1994] The sound of breaking glass: also CRASHH [Dare Devil: The Man Without Fear vol.1 #3, 1993] The sound of ice breaking: [Dare Devil: The Man Without Fear vol.1 #5, 1994] The sound of a collision: [Steel #1.1994] A crashing sound, as of metal garbage cans falling over: [Archie #407, 1993] A crashing sound, as often heard while playing an arcade game: [The Adventures of Toucan Sam, 1994] The sound of falling fruit
CRASHH see CRASH
CREAAK also CREEAK [Ripley's Believe It Or Not: True Ghost Stories #53, 1975] A creaking sound
CREEAK see CREAAK
CREEEEK [MAD #188, January 1977] The sound of a drawbridge opening
CRICK CRACK [MAD Super Special 16, 1975] The sound of knuckles being cracked
CROOOM [Mantra vol.1 #2, 1993] The sound of an explosion
CRRR [The Adventures of Tintin: Explorers on the Moon, 1954] The sound of radio static
CRRUNCH see CRUNCH
CRRUNCH [Son of MAD, 1973] The sound of a boat wreck: [Madballs vol.1 #7, 1987] A sound made by a tank
CRSHK [Dare Devil #277] A crashing sound
CRUMP [The Vision and The Scarlet Witch vol.2 #7, 1986] The sound of a body hitting the floor
CRUNCH [MAD #211, December 1979] The sound of a collision: [MAD #244, January 1984] The sound of a punch: [Dare Devil: The Man Without Fear vol.1 #3, 1993] A crunching sound: [Venom: The Enemy Within #2, 1994] The sound of a hole being punched through solid concrete: also CRUNNCHHH [Venom: The Enemy Within #2, 1994] A punching sound
CRUNNCHHH see CRUNCH

CRZZPT [Mantra: Infinity, 1995] The sound of an electronic discharge
DANG [MAD #215, June 1980] The sound of a fire truck bell
DASH [The Twisted Tantrum of the Purple Snit #1, 1980] A sound of people and equipment in operation, as might be heard on a construction site
D-DING [MAD #227, December 1981] A sound from a pinball machine
DEET [Hawkeye vol.2 #3, 1994] The sound of a high frequency transmission, in this case from the Secret Empire
DING [MAD #212, January 1980] The sound of a pumping machine: [MAD #227, December 1981] A sound from a pinball machine
DINGALINGA [MAD #223, June 1981] also DINGILINGA [MAD #252, January 1985] The sound of a bell being rung
DING DONG [The Vision and The Scarlet Witch vol.2 #7, 1986] The sound of a doorbell: [Madballs vol.1 #7, 1987] The sound of a bell, as those often seen on hotel reception desks
DING GING [MAD #227, December 1981] A sound from a pinball machine
DINGG [War Machine vol.1 #1, 1994] The sound of an elevator floor indicator bell
DINGILINGA see DINGALINGA
DINK-DINK-DINK-DINK [MAD's Don Martin Cooks Up More Tales, 1976] The sound made by a spring board
DIT [MAD #177, September 1975] The sound of a falling hat hitting a head
D'OH [Mantra vol.1 #5, 1993] An expression similar in function to a mild oath or curse
DOINK [The Anomalies #1, 2000] A sound made by a head hitting the ground
DOOM [2099 Unlimited vol.1 #2, 1993] The sound of an explosion
DOON [The Twisted Tantrum of the Purple Snit #1, 1980] A sound of people and equipment in operation, as might be heard on a construction site
DOOOT [MAD #244, January 1984] The sound of a work whistle
DRRRRIIINNNNGGG [Detective Comics vol.47 #529, 1983] The sound of an alarm bell
DUBDUBDUBDUBDUBDUB [MAD #215, June 1980] The sound of a helicopter
DUM-TI-DUM [MAD #231, June 1982] The sound of dramatic TV music

DUNT [The Night Man vol.1 #4, 1994] A sound of a heel hitting cement
DWAT [Mantra vol.1 #5, 1993] Means "Drat", a mild curse or oath
DWEE [2099 Unlimited vol.1 #3, 1993] The sound of a bullet in flight
Editor's note: Comic words beginning with E are often vocalizations of pain and suffering.
EEE [New Kids On The Block: Step By Step, 1990] A cry of delight
EEEAGGHHHH [Venom: The Enemy Within vol.1 #1, 1994] A ghostly wailing sound
EEEE [Mantra vol.1 #7, 1994] A cry of pain
EEEECCHH [The Adventures of Bayou Billy #4, 1990] A screeching sound, as of brakes: [Mantra vol.1 #7, 1994] A cry of pain
EEEEE [2099 Unlimited vol.1 #3, 1993] A cry of terror
EEEEEE [MAD #225, September 1981] The sound of a smoke alarm: [Dare Devil: The Man Without Fear vol.1 #5, 1994] also EEEEEEEE [Dare Devil: The Man Without Fear vol.1 #2, 1993] The sound of a police siren
EEE-EE-EE [Secret Origins DC vol.2 #7] The diminishing cry of a falling person
EEEEEEE [Madballs vol.1 #7, 1987] The sound of a scream
EEEEEEEE see EEEEEE
EEEEEEEEEE [Venom: The Enemy Within #2, 1994] The sound of a brain piercing wail: also EEEEEEEEEEEEE also EEEEEEEEEEEEEEE also EEEEEEEEEEEEEEEEEE [Venom: The Enemy Within vol.1 #1, 1994] A wailing sound; A scream of terror: also EEEE-EE-EEE-EE also EE-EEE-EEEE-EE [New Kids On The Block: Magic Summer Tour, 1990] The sound of screaming crowds
EEEE-EE-EEE-EE see EEEEEEEEEE
EE-EEE-EEEE-EE see EEEEEEEEEE
EEEEEEEEEEEEE see EEEEEEEEEE
EEEEEEEEEEEEEEE see EEEEEEEEEE
EEEEEEEEEEEEEEEEEE see EEEEEEEEEE
EEEEHAUGHHH [Venom: The Enemy Within vol.1 #1, 1994] The sound of a sonic blast
EeeEEKK [Mantra vol.1 #2, 1993] A cry of fear; A scream
EEEEK [MAD #222, April 1981] A cry of fear
EEEEYAAAAH [The Ren and Stimpy Show vol.1 #6, 1993] A sound made by a person straining physically
EEEK see EEK

EEE-OOOOOOO [The Adventures of Bayou Billy #3, 1990] A wailing animal sound

EEEUW [Betty #40] A sound made to express disgust or dislike

EEEYOWW [Betty #40] A cry of surprise, protest, discomfort or pain; also EEYAAA [X-Factor vol.1 #84, 1992] also EEYAGH also EEYARGH [ROM #35, 1982] also EEYARGX [Ralph Snart Adventures vol.5, 1993] A cry of pain

EEE-YUK [The Adventures of Bayou Billy #4, 1990] An exclamation of disgust

EEK also EEEK [New Kids On The Block: Magic Summer Tour, 1990] A cry of delight

EEP [New Kids On The Block: Step By Step, 1990] A beeping sound made by a telephone: [Hawkeye vol.2 #2, 1994] A squeaky exclamation: also eep [Mantra: Infinity, 1995] A small gasping sound

eep see EEP

EEYAAA see EEEYOWW

EEYAGH see EEEYOWW

EEYARGH see EEEYOWW

EEYARGX see EEEYOWW

ERGHHH [Captain Atom #7] A gurgling or groaning sound

EXPWESS [Mantra vol.1 #5, 1993] Means "Express"

Editor's note: Comic words beginning with F are most often related to swift, sudden motion.

FAASSH [The Solution 5] A flashing sound

FACHOW [Cable 5, 1993] The sound of an energy beam hitting the ground

FAGROOLANA [MAD #249, September 1984] The sound in a morgue of a body cabinet drawer opening

FAH-BHAMMM [The Adventures of Bayou Billy #4, 1990] The sound of a collision

FAK [The Adventures of Bayou Billy #3, 1990] The sound of an arrow's shaft breaking: [The Adventures of Bayou Billy #4, 1990] The sound of a weapon being knocked out of a hand

FAM [The Night Man vol.1 #4, 1994] The sound of a stone door closing

FAP [Clint: The Hamster Triumphant #1, 1986] The sound made by hitting a large sheet of paper

FAPP [Dare Devil: The Man Without Fear vol.1 #4, 1994] The sound of a punch to a workout bag

FASH [Dead Pool: The Circle Chase 4, 1993] The sound of an energy blast

FASHOOM [The Twisted Tantrum of the Purple Snit #1, 1980] A sound of people and equipment in operation, as might be heard on a construction site
FASHUNK [MAD #249, September 1984] The sound of a morgue body cabinet drawer closing
FA-WHUMP [The Adventures of Bayou Billy #3, 1990] The sound of bodies in collision
FAZ [Captain Marvel vol.1 #42, 1976] The sound of an energy bolt
FEEOOOT [MAD's Don Martin Cooks Up More Tales, 1976] The musical sound of a dowsing stick when it finds water
FEEOOP [MAD's Don Martin Cooks Up More Tales, 1976] The sound of a person jumping off a parapet
FEEP [Star Hunters vol.2 #4, 1978] The sound made by a switch: [New Kids On The Block: Step By Step, 1990] The sound of a telephone
FERRIP [MAD #218, October 1980] The sound of a deck of cards being riffled
FERSPLASH [Knights of Pendragon 13] A splashing sound
FFF FFFT [Clint #1, 1986] The sound of an airborne object in motion
FFFT [MAD #224, January 1981] The sound of a boxing glove to the face: [Dakota North vol.1 #3, 1986] The sound of a handgun with a silencer: also ffft [Mantra vol.1 #5, 1993] A sound accompanying a sudden disappearance
ffft see FFFT
FFRZZAAK [Darkhold 10, 1993] The sound of an electrical discharge
FFFFSST [MAD #202, December 1978] The sound of a fire extinguisher
FFFRRRAAPFT [MAD Super Special Number 31, Summer 1980] The sound made by an inflated body rapidly deflating as it flies through the air like a balloon
FFT [Catwoman 6, 1994] The sound made by the deployment of wrist cable
FFZT [Madballs vol.1 #7, 1987] The sound made by a "Piece Maker" rocket ignition
FITZROWER [MAD #211, December 1979] A fighting cry
FIZZ [Dead Pool: The Circle Chase 4, 1993] A sound made when mechanical parts come undone
FIZZAZZIT [MAD #223, June 1981] The sound of a spray can being sprayed
FIZZZ [Madballs vol.1 #7, 1987] A fizzing sound, as from a chemical pond of toxic waste

FLADIP [MAD #252, January 1985] The sound of an object falling into a slot
FLADOINNG [MAD #223, June 1981] The sound of a spring loaded lens cap coming off
FLAMM [The Vision and The Scarlet Witch vol.2 #7, 1986] The sound of an object being destroyed by an electronic field
FLANG [2099 Unlimited vol.1 #4, 1993] A metallic hitting sound
FLAPTAPTAP [Mantra vol.1 #5, 1993] A sound of an object rolling itself up quickly
FLASH [Madballs vol.1 #7, 1987] A sudden bright light of short duration, in this case, coming from a Cosmic Camera
FLICK [Madballs vol.1 #7, 1987] The sound made while removing the ash accumulating on a cigar end
FLIK [MAD #218, October 1980] The sound of a playing card: [MAD #227, December 1981] The sound of a single card being taken from a fanned deck: [MAD #249, September 1984] The sound of a fifty dollar bill being plucked from a john's hand: [The Adventures of Bayou Billy #2, 1989] The sound of a lighter on a flame thrower
F-LOP [New Kids On The Block: Magic Summer Tour, 1990] The sound of a body falling to the ground
FLSSH [Knights of Pendragon 13] A splashing sound
FLUTCH [Star Hunters vol.2 #5, 1978] The deployment sound of an organic detection device
FLOIP [MAD #217, September 1980] The sound of an object being pulled out of a mouth
floof [MAD #181, March 1976] A word indicating a puff of smoke has appeared, as in a smoke signal: also FLOOF [MAD #181, March 1976] The imaginary sound of a single puff of smoke created with a blanket
floof floofity flif flif flof daflaf [MAD #181, March 1976] The imaginary sounds of an entire smoke signal communication (translation unknown)
FLUMMP [MAD #188, January 1977] The sound of a shark jumping out of the water and onto a surfboard
FLUP [Son of MAD, 1973] The sound of a head being pulled inside out
FOOF [Prototype vol.1 #6, 1994] The sound of a hermetic seal failing
FOOM [MAD #177, September 1975] The sound of a super hero crashing through a wall: [The Twisted Tantrum of the Purple Snit #1, 1980] A sound of people and equipment in operation, as might be heard on a construction site: [Cold Blooded Chamelion Commando #1, 1986] The sound made by

a rocket launcher firing: [Steel #1.1994] The sound of a large gun firing
FOOMP [The Ren and Stimpy Show vol.1, 6, 1993] A distress call
FLOON [MAD's Don Martin Cooks Up More Tales, 1976] The sound of a body thrown from a height and hitting the ground: [MAD #238, April 1983] The sound of a radiator exploding
FOOOM [MAD #211, December 1979] The sound of a truck load of popcorn exploding
FOOOOSH [Madballs vol.1 #7, 1987] A sound made by blowing a stream of smoke
FOOSH [2099 Unlimited vol.1 #3, 1993] The sound of an energy blast
FOP [The Adventures of Bayou Billy #3, 1989] The sound of an exploding knockout gas canister
FPP [Dare Devil: The Man Without Fear vol.1 #5, 1994] The sound made while catching a coin in mid air
FRAAK [Avengers West Coast Annual vol.2 #8, 1993] The sound of an energy bolt hitting the ground
FRAP [The Ren and Stimpy Show 6, 1993] The simulated fart sound made with one hand cupped under the opposite armpit, as any boy can instantly demonstrate
FROOM [Star Wars Vol.1 #6 1977] The sound of an explosion
FROOOOSH also FROOSH [Son of MAD, 1973] The imaginary sound of a cold draft of air when a door opens
FROOOSH [Avengers West Coast Annual vol.2 #8, 1993] A sound of an energy bolt
FROOSH see FROOOOSH
FRUNK [Knights of Pendragon 13] A hitting sound
fSHOOM also f-SHOOOOOOM [FREEX #7, 1994] A sound of an energy bolt
f-SHOOOOOOM see fSHOOM
FSHPLAP [MAD's Don Martin Cooks Up More Tales, 1976] The sound of a skydiver hitting a spring board
FSHSSSTTT [Dead Pool: The Circle Chase 4, 1993] The burning sound of a magnesium flare
FSSHH [2099 Unlimited vol.1 #2, 1993] The sound of a rapidly moving air vehicle
FSSSIP [The Ren and Stimpy Show vol.1 #6, 1993] The sound made by a jet of liquid from a hose hitting a target
FSSTTTTT [The Adventures of Bayou Billy #4, 1990] A welding torch sound
FTHOOM [Captain Thunder and Blue Bolt 1] A sound made when an electrical bolt strikes an object

FTOOM [Star Wars Vol.1 #6 1977] The sound of an explosion
FUD [Ralph Snart Adventures vol.5, 1993] A punching sound
FUH-WHOOM [The Adventures of Bayou Billy #2, 1989] The sound of an explosion
FUMP [The Adventures of Bayou Billy #3, 1989] The sound of a body falling to the ground: [The Adventures of Bayou Billy #4, 1990] The sound of an exploding gas canister: [Dare Devil: The Man Without Fear vol.1 #2, 1993] A jumping sound
FUP [Clint #1, 1986] The sound of gunfire
FUPP [Dare Devil: The Man Without Fear vol.1 #4, 1994] The sound of a gunshot: [Dare Devil: The Man Without Fear vol.1 #5, 1994] The sound of a head smashing into a windshield
FWA-BOK [2099 Unlimited vol.1 #4, 1993] A punching sound
FWACH [MAD #229, March 1982] A sweeping sound
FWACKT [Cold Blooded Chamelion Commando #1, 1986] The sound of hit
FWAK [MAD's Don Martin Cooks Up More Tales, 1976] The sound of a telephone being seized: [The Solution vol.1 #2, 1993] A kicking sound: [2099 Unlimited vol.1 #3, 1993] A hitting sound
FWAKOOM [Gambit vol.1 #1, 1993] The sound of an explosion
FWAP [The Adventures of Bayou Billy #3, 1989] The sound of a slap
FWAT [Mantra vol.1 #5, 1993] Means "Flat"
FWATHOOM [The Ren and Stimpy Show vol.1, 6, 1993] The sound of an energy bolt
FWEE [MAD #177, September 1975] The imaginary sound of a hat being blown off
FWEEEEE [MAD #212, January 1980] The sound of Spiderman swinging from his web cord
FWHEEEEE [The Ren and Stimpy Show vol.1, 6, 1993] A sound, as that of air escaping from a balloon
FWIBTHH [2099 Unlimited vol.1 #3, 1993] A hitting sound
FWIP [The Twisted Tantrum of the Purple Snit #1, 1980] The sound of a fast swiping action: [The Ren and Stimpy Show vol.1, 6, 1993] The deployment sound of Spiderman's web fluid
FWISK [MAD's Don Martin Cooks Up More Tales, 1976] The sound of a quick whisking action

FWISKITTY FWASK [MAD #229, March 1982] The sound of sweeping back and forth rapidly

FWIZZACH [MAD #229, March 1982] A sweeping sound

FWOOM [Clint #1, 1986] The sound of an explosion: [The Solution vol.1 #2, 1993] The sound of an energy bolt: also FWOOOM [Mantra vol.1 #5, 1993] The sound of a non-physical entity taking instantaneous physical form

FWOOOM see FWOOM

FWOOOOSH see FWOOSH

FWOOOSH see FWOOSH

FWOOSH [MAD #218, October 1980] The sound made by swinging a tennis racquet: [MAD #232, July 1982] The sound of water being sprayed by a hose: [Madballs vol.1 #7, 1987] A rising, rushing sound: [Mantra vol.1 #5, 1993] The sound of a magical force being transmitted: also FWOOOSH [Mantra vol.1 #5, 1993] A rushing sound: also FWOOOOSH [The Solution vol.1 #2, 1993] The sound of an energy bolt

FWOP [2099 Unlimited vol.1 #2, 1993] A sound made by a trap door swinging open

FWROOSH [ROM34, 1982] The sound of a house erupting in flames

FWUD [Knights of Pendragon 13] The sound made by a body hitting the ground

FWUMP [The Adventures of Bayou Billy #2, 1989] A kicking sound

FWZAAM [X-Factor vol.1 #84, 1992] The sound of an explosion

FZOOOOOSH [Madballs vol.1 37, 1987] The sound of a rocket in flight

FZSSSSSSSSSS [MAD #217, September 1980] The sound of champagne fizzing

FZZ [Dead Pool: The Circle Chase 4, 1993] The sound of mechanical parts coming undone

FZZAKKL [FREEX #7, 1994] A sound made when entering cyberspace

FZZASH [Star Hunters vol.2 #5, 1978] The sound of electronic weapon fire

FZZT [Dead Pool: The Circle Chase 4, 1993] The sound of a body being hit with an energy blast

FZZZRATCH [Star Hunters vol.2 35, 1978] The sound of electronic weapon fire

FZZZT also **FZZZZT** [Superboy #154, 1969] The sound of an object suddenly breaking into flames: also FZZZZT [Avengers West Coast Annual vol.2 #8, 1993] The sound of a force field

FZZZZ [Avengers West Coast Annual vol.2 #8, 1993] The sound made by an energy beam
FZZZZL [Avengers West Coast Annual vol.2 #8, 1993] The sound of electricity
FZZZZT see FZZZT
FZZZZZ [Star Hunters vol.2 #4, 1978] The sound of armament banks freezing up: [Avengers West Coast Annual vol.2 #8, 1993] The sound of an energy bolt
FZZZZZZZZZ [Avengers West Coast Annual vol.2 #8, 1993] The sound of an energy blast
GAA [Dare Devil: The Man Without Fear vol.1 #4, 1994] A cry of pain
GAAAH [Mantra vol.1 #2, 1993] A cry of pain: [Archie #407, 1993] A cry of fear
GAACCK [MAD #227, December 1981] The sound of gagging
GADANG also GADOING also GLOING also GOING [MAD Super Special Number 31, Summer 1980] The sound made by bouncing on a coil spring
GADOING see GADANG
GADONG [MAD #177, September 1975] The sound of a wedding bell
GAG [MAD #229, March 1982] An accompanying sound to laughter
gagg [MAD #177, September 1975] The sound of a person gagging over bug spray
GAGG [Son of MAD, 1973] also Gaggh.... [MAD #212, January 1980] A gagging sound
GAGGAK-THOOF [MAD's Don Martin Cooks Up More Tales, 1976] The sound of a beetle being spit out
Gaggh.... see GAGG
GAHAK [MAD #175, June 1975] The sound of a final hacking cough
GAK [MAD #175, June 1975] The sound emitted by a dying person; The sound of a throat being cleared
GAKKK [Thunderstrike vol.1 #4, 1994] A cry of pain
GALOON [MAD #177, September 1975] The sound of a wedding bell
GAPLORK [MAD #233, September 1982] A sound of soup
GARR [Dare Devil: The Man Without Fear vol.1 #5, 1994] A cry of pain
GARRGH [MAD #221, March 1981] The sound of a normal sized body morphing to a larger one
GASHKLITZKA [MAD #225, September 1981] also **GASHLITZGA** [MAD #219, December 1980] The sound of a plastic lapel flower spraying water

GASHLIKT [MAD #229, March 1982] The sound of a sculptor working with a plastic material

GASHLITZGA see GASHKLITZKA

GASP [MAD #175, June 1975] The sound emitted by a dying person

GDONG [The Ren and Stimpy Show vol.1 #6, 1993] The sound that a pipe makes when struck against another object

GEEEEEZ [Darkhold: Pages From The Book of Sins vol.1 #7, 1993] Signifies G-Forces

GEEN GEEN [MAD #215, June 1980] The sound of a coil spring decompressing

GEEP [New Kids On The Block: Step By Step, 1990] A sound made by a telephone

GEHHHH [Dare Devil: The Man Without Fear vol.1 #4, 1994] A groaning sound

GGGRRR also GGGRRRAAA [The Ren and Stimpy Show vol.1 #6, 1993] A sound made by a person straining physically

GGGRRRAAA see GGGRRR

GGGRRRR [The Adventures of Bayou Billy #3, 1990] A growling sound

GING [MAD's Don Martin Cooks Up More Tales, 1976] The sound of a spring board being tensioned: [MAD #244, January 1984] The sound of an elastic stretching

GING GING [MAD #231, June 1982] The sound of a jack-in-the-box popping out, except that it's a person's stomach

GINK [MAD's Don Martin Cooks Up More Tales, 1976] The sound of a spring board being tensioned

GLABADAP [MAD #233, September 1982] The sound of bodies in collision

GLAGGG [Dare Devil: The Man Without Fear vol.1 #2, 1993] A gurgling sound

GLAKK [Dare Devil: The Man Without Fear vol.1 #4, 1994] A strangling sound

GLANGADANG [MAD #177, September 1975] The sound of wedding bells

GLARRR [Clint #1, 1986] An alien word meaning "OK, now I'm ticked"

GLAWK [MAD Super Special Number 31, Summer 1980] The sound made by a bird being force fed

GLEEP [MAD #217, September 1980] The sound of a bad bird call: [New Kids On The Block: Step By Step, 1990] A sound made by a telephone

GLING [MAD's Don Martin Cooks Up More Tales, 1976] The sound of a beetle that has hit a fan at full speed

GLIP [MAD #233, September 1982] The sound of soup

GLiT [MAD #224, January 1981] A gulping sound smaller than a GLUK
GLIT [MAD #233, September 1982] The sound of soup
GLITCH [MAD #230, April 1982] A video game sound indicating an error
GLOING see GADANG
GLOMP [MAD #249, September 1984] An eating sound
GLONG [MAD #177, September 1975] The sound of a wedding bell
GLOOCHLE [MAD #229, March 1982] The sound of a sculptor working with a plastic material
GLOOP [MAD #211, December 1979] The sound of food being splashed: [MAD #233, September 1982] The sound of soup
GLORP [MAD #211, December 1979] The sound of food being splashed: [The Adventures of Bayou Billy #4, 1990] Bubble sounds as those made when a head is held under water against its owner's will
GLUB [The Adventures of Bayou Billy #2, 1989] The sound made by a person blowing a bubble under water: [The Adventures of Bayou Billy #4, 1990] Bubble sounds as those made when a head is held under water against its owner's will
GLUG [Darkhold: Pages From The Book of Sins vol.1 #7, 1993] A gurgling sound
GLUG-GLUG [Madballs vol.1 #7, 1987] A drinking sound
GLUK [MAD #224, January 1981] A gulping sound
GLUMP [ROM #34, 1982] A swallowing sound
GLUMPH see GLUMP
GLUP [MAD #233, September 1982] The sound of soup: [The Adventures of Bayou Billy #4, 1990] Bubble sounds as those made when a head is held under water against its owner's will
GLUTCH [MAD #229, March 1982] The sound of a sculptor working with a plastic material
GNAA [Dare Devil: The Man Without Fear vol.1 #5, 1994] The sound made by a car ignition turning over without firing
GNAAAAAR [Hawkeye vol.2 #2, 1994] A snarling, roaring cry
GOBBLE GOBBLE [Archie #407, 1993] The sound a turkey makes
GOING [MAD's Don Martin Cooks Up More Tales, 1976] The sound of a spring board being tensioned
GONG [MAD's Don Martin Cooks Up More Tales, 1976] The sound of a bell ringing
GONK [MAD #233, September 1982] The sound of bodies in collision

GORE [MAD #212, January 1980] The sound made by a person being strangled

GOTCHA [Mantra vol.1 #5, 1993] Means "(I) Got you", understand

GRAAHH [The Solution vol.1 #2, 1993] A cry of rage

GRING [MAD Super Special 16, 1975] The sound of a telephone ringing

GROARR [The Adventures of Bayou Billy #3, 1990] A roaring sound, as made by an animal

GROON [MAD #202, December 1978] A mechanical sound formed at a joint

GRONK [Star Wars Vol.1 #6 1977] A sound made by Chewbacca

GROWL... [The Adventures of Kool-Aid Man #6, 1989] A growling sound

GRR... see GRRR

GRRARR [The Incredible Hulk vol.1 #226, 1978] A growling sound

GRRR also GRR [MAD #233, September 1982]: also GRRR [MAD #233, September 1982]: also GRRR... [MAD #227, December 1981]: also GRRRR [MAD #224, January 1981]: also GRRRR... [MAD #227, December 1981]: also GRRRRRR... [MAD #219, December 1980] The sound of a dog growl: [MAD #241, September 1983]: GRRRRRR [MAD #241, September 1983] The sound of a hacksaw: Grrrrr [MAD #225, September 1981] A growling sound signifying anger: [G.I.Joe vol.1 #60, 1987] also GRR... [The Adventures of Kool-Aid Man #6, 1989] also GRRRRRR [The Adventures of Bayou Billy #3, 1990] also GRRRRRRRR [The Adventures of Bayou Billy #3, 1989] A growling sound: also GRRR... also GRRRR also GR-R-R-R [Superboy #154, 1969] also GRRRRR [G.I.Joe vol.1 #60, 1987] The growling of a dog

GRR see GRRR

GRRR... see GRRR

GRRRGUK [Catwoman #6, 1994] A sound made by a blade slicing through flesh

GRRRR see GRRR

GRRRR... see GRRR

GR-R-R-R see GRRR

GRRRRR see GRRR

GRRRRRR see GRRR

GRRRRRR... see GRRR

GRRRRRRR see GRRRGUK

GRUNCH [MAD #229, March 1982] The sound of a sculptor working with a plastic material

GULP [MAD #233, September 1982] A drinking sound: [MAD #249, September 1984] An eating sound

GURGG see GURGLE

GURGLE [Madballs vol.1 #7, 1987] A gurgling sound, as heard near a toxic waste chemical pond: GURGG [Captain Atom #7] A gurgling sound

GWAP [MAD #246, April 1984] The sound of a dog biting a person's nose

GWARRR [X-Factor vol.1 #84, 1992] A roar

GYAAAARHHH [Wonderman #12, 1992] A cry of pain or anguish

GZZZT [Star Hunters vol.2 #4, 1978] The sound of electronic weapon fire hitting metal

HA [MAD #229, March 1982] also HA HA HA HA HA HA [Captain Atom #7] also HAAAHAAA [The Solution #5] also HAH [MAD #229, March 1982] also HAR [Madballs vol.1 #7, 1987] also HAHAHAHAHA [New Kids On The Block: Step By Step, 1990] also HA HA HAHO HA HOOT HOO HA HA also HA-HA also HA-HAHAHA [The Adventures of Bayou Billy #2, 1989] also HAHAHA [Mantra vol.1 #2, 1993] also HAHA [Mantra: Infinity, 1995] The sound of laughter

HAAAAR [MAD #209, September 1979] A martial arts cry

HAAAHAAA see HA

HACK-GACK-IKLE-SHLIK [MAD's Don Martin Cooks Up More Tales, 1976] The sound of sectioning, slicing, trimming and grinding of meat

HAH see HA

HAHA see HA

HA-HA see HA

HAHAHA see HA

HA-HAHAHA see HA

HAHAHAHAHA see HA

HA HA HA HA HA HA see HA

HA HA HAHO HA HOOT HOO HA HA see HA

HAI also HAII [Clint #1, 1986] A cry

HAII see HAI

HAIII [Cold Blooded Chamelion Commando #1, 1986] A martial arts cry

HAK-GASP [MAD's Don Martin Cooks Up More Tales, 1976] The struggling sound of a dying man

HALLLPYAAAAA [MAD #227, December 1981] A cry of fear emerging from a cry for help

HAR see HA

HAUGGHHHHH [Venom: The Enemy Within #2, 1994] also HAUGGHHHHHMM also HAUUGGGGHHHHHHHH also

HAUUGGGHHHHHHH [Venom: The Enemy Within vol.1 #1, 1994] The sound of a sonic blast
HAUGGHHHHHMM see HAUGGHHHHH
HAUUGGGHHHHHHHH see HAUGGHHHHH
HAUUGGGHHHHHHH see HAUGGHHHHH
HAYYY YAHH [MAD #227, December 1981] A martial arts cry
HEE [MAD #229, March 1982] also HEEEEEEEE [MAD #241, September 1983] The sound of laughter
HEEEEEEEE see HEE
HEE-HEE [Bobby Sherman #6, 1972] The sounds of giggling or laughter
HEHEHEHE see HEH-HEH
HEHEHEHEHE see HEH-HEH
HEH-HEH also HEH-HEH-HEH-HEH-HEH [Venom: The Enemy Within vol.1 #1, 1994] also HEHEHEHE also HEHEHEHEHE [Mantra vol.1 #5, 1993] The sound of laughter: see HA
HEH-HEH-HEH-HEH-HEH see HEH-HEH
HEP [Son of MAD, 1973] The sound Mounties make with each step
HEY-YY [Betty #40] An exclamation of surprise or disagreement
HHEYUUHHHH also HHHRURRR [The Ren and Stimpy Show vol.1 #6, 1993] A sound made by a person straining physically
HHUURGG [Dare Devil: The Man Without Fear vol.1 #3, 1993] A strangling sound
HHUYECHH [The Ren and Stimpy Show vol.1 #6, 1993] A sound expressing disgust, dislike etc
HIC [MAD #177, September 1975] The sound of a hiccough
HII-YAAAH [The Twisted Tantrum of the Purple Snit #1, 1980] The sound of a martial arts cry
HISSS [Dare Devil: The Man Without Fear vol.1 #2, 1993] The sound of a cat hiss: also HISSSSSS [ROM #43, 1983] A prolonged hissing sound
HISSSSSS see HISSS
HISSSST [The Adventures of Bayou Billy #2, 1989] The sound of gas escaping from its canister
HMMM [The Ren and Stimpy Show vol.1 #6, 1993] also HMMMM [MAD Super Special 16, 1975] also Hmmmmm... [MAD's Don Martin Cooks Up More Tales, 1976] also HMMMMM... [G.I.Joe vol.1 #60, 1987] A humming sound used to express or signify a thought process in progress
MMMM see HMMM

Hmmmmm... see HMMM
Hmmmmm... see HMMM
HMMMMM... see HMMM
HMMMMPH [Betty #40] A sound made to express contempt
HNH? [Dare Devil: The Man Without Fear vol.1 #3, 1993] A sound signifying a question, as "Huh?" or "What?"
HNNN [Mantra: Infinity, 1995] A grunting sound, as when hit
HNNNGNN [Avengers West Coast Annual vol.2 #8, 1993] A cry of pain
HO [MAD #229, March 1982] HO HO HA HA HEE HO [Star Hunters vol.2 #4, 1978] also HOO-HA HA HA HA HA HA [The Adventures of Bayou Billy #2, 1989] The sounds of laughter: see HA
HO HO HA HA HEE HO see HO
HONK! HONK! [Monkey Shines of Marseleen, 1906] The sound of a car horn
HOO [MAD #241, September 1983] The sound of laughter
HOO HAA [Son of MAD, 1973] The sound of a scornful laugh
HOO-HA HA HA HA HA HA see HO HO HA HA HEE HO
HOOP [Son of MAD, 1973] The sound made by a person having his breath knocked out
HOORAY [MAD #177, September 1975] A cheering exclamation of admiration
HOOT [New Kids On The Block: Magic Summer Tour, 1990] The cry of an owl
hrn? [Mantra vol.1 #7, 1994] An interrogative sound that means "Huh?" or "What?"
HUKK [Dare Devil: The Man Without Fear vol.1 #3, 1993] The sound of the last breath of a dying man; A sound made as the throat is blocked to respiration
HUMMMMM [MAD's Don Martin Cooks Up More Tales, 1976] The sound of an airplane heard from a distance
HURRRRR [2099 Unlimited vol.1 #4, 1993] A roaring sound
HWOKSH [Batman #502, 1993] The sound of a head being kicked
HYUK [The Twisted Tantrum of the Purple Snit #1, 1980] A sound of laughter
iFFFFPFP [MAD's Don Martin Cooks Up More Tales, 1976] The sound of a tuba player sucking in air
INGALINGALINGALINGALING [FREEX #7, 1994] The sounds of an alarm
I-YI-YI [Clint: The Hamster Triumphant #1, 1986] An expression of surprise, wonderment etc

JEEZ [The Night Man vol.1 #4, 1994] An exclamation of surprise etc used as a euphemism for Jesus

Editor's note: Comic words beginning with K are often related to explosive sounds. KA- and variations such as KE- or KER- are used to intensify the basic sound effect.

KAA-POW see KAPOW

KAA-RUUNNCH [The Twisted Tantrum of the Purple Snit #1, 1980] A loud crunching sound

KAA-WHUUMPH [The Twisted Tantrum of the Purple Snit #1, 1980] The sound of a body hitting the ground

KA-BAM [The Adventures of Bayou Billy #4, 1990] The sound of a gunshot

KABASH [The Twisted Tantrum of the Purple Snit #1, 1980] A hitting sound

KABLOOM [MAD #217, September 1980] The sound of an explosion

KA-BOOM [The Incredible Hulk vol.1 #229, 1978] The sound of an explosion: also KA-BOOOOM [G.I.Joe vol.1 #61, 1987] also KA-BOOOMM also KA-BOOOMMMM [Captain Atom #7] The sound of an explosion

KA-BOOOMM see KA-BOOM

KA-BOOOMMMM see KA-BOOM

KA CHOOM [The Adventures of Bayou Billy #3, 1989] The sound of an exploding nerve gas canister: also KA-CHOOM [The Solution vol.1 #2, 1993] The sound of an explosion

KA-CHOOM see KA CHOOM

KACHONK [MAD #244, January 1984] A hitting sound

KACHUNK [MAD #177, September 1975] The sound of an object like a cartridge being ejected from a magazine

KACK [The Adventures of Bayou Billy #2, 1989] The sound of a flame thrower

KADOONK [MAD #249, September 1984] The sound of a prison guard slam dunking meat loaf into a prisoner's mouth

KADOOM [The Solution vol.1 #2, 1993] The sound of an explosion

KA-DOONK [MAD #181, March 1976] The sound of a seeing eye dog walking into a telephone pole

KAFF [The Adventures of Bayou Billy #3, 1989] also KAFF-KAFF [Venom: The Enemy Within #2, 1994] A coughing sound

KAFF-KAFF see KAFF

KAHAK also KAHIKE [MAD #175, June 1975] The sound of hacking cough

KAHIKE see KAHAK

KAKK [Dare Devil: The Man Without Fear vol.1 #3, 1993] A kicking sound
KAPF [MAD #175, June 1975] The sound of a cough
KA POKK also KA-POKK also KA-POKK!POKK [Detective Comics vol.47 #529, 1983] The sound of an exploding spray canister
KA-POKK see KA POKK
KA-POKK!POKK see KA POKK
KAPOW [Our Fighting Forces #111, 1968] The sound of a tank gun: [Ultraman vol.1 #2, 1994] A hitting sound: also KAPOWW [Detective Comics vol.47 #529, 1983] The sound of an explosion: KAA-POW [Ultraman vol.1 #1, 1994] The sound of a gunshot
KAPOWW see KAPOW
KAPTHOOM [Dead Pool: The Circle Chase #4, 1993] A punching sound
KARASH [Superboy #154, 1969]: also KARASHH [The Anomalies #1, 2000] A crashing sound
KARASHBOOMBAM [The Twisted Tantrum of the Purple Snit #1, 1980] A sound of people and equipment in operation, as might be heard on a construction site
KARASHH see KARASH
KA ROOOOM [2099 Unlimited vol.1 #3, 1993] The sound of a shattering blow
KA-ROOOOOSH [G.I.Joe vol.1 #61, 1987] The sound of a speeding vehicle colliding with other vehicles
KA-RUMP [The Adventures of Bayou Billy #2, 1989] The sound of an explosion
KASH [The Twisted Tantrum of the Purple Snit #1, 1980] A sound of people and equipment in operation, as might be heard on a construction site
KASHH [Dare Devil: The Man Without Fear vol.1 #2, 1993] The sound of a breaking glass
KA-SPANG [Iron Man #277, 1992] The sound of magnetic grapples
KATCHOOM [MAD #212, January 1980] The sound of a massive collision
KA-THRASH [G.I.Joe vol.1 #60, 1987] The sound of a collision
KATL [The Night Man vol.1 #4, 1994] A breaking sound
KATOOF [MAD #215, June 1980] The sound of a flare gun
KATOOOM [Warlock vol.2 #3, 1992] The sound of an explosion
KATOOOSH [Warlock vol.2 #3, 1992] The sound of an energy beam being deployed

KATRANG [The Adventures of Bayou Billy #4, 1990] The sound of a collision: [Thunderstrike vol.1 #4, 1994] A metallic banging sound, as of an ax hitting a shield
KAW also **KAWW** [Dare Devil: The Man Without Fear vol.1 #2, 1993] The sound of a bird's cry
KAWHUMP [The Adventures of Bayou Billy #3, 1990] The sound of a falling body hitting a car
KA-WHOOOM [Thunderstrike vol.1 #2, 1994] The sound of an explosion
KAWW see KAW
KAZAK [The Solution #5] An electrical sound caused by overload
K-BAM [Captain Marvel vol.1 #42, 1976] A hitting, smashing sound
KCHOOM [NFL SuperPro vol.1 #9, 1992] A zooming sound
KCHOW [2099 Unlimited vol.1 #2, 1993] The sound of weapon fire
K-CHUNK [MAD #188, January 1977] The sound of a bullet in the back
KEE-RASH [G.I.Joe vol.1 #104, 1990] also **KERAASH** [Darkhold #10, 1993] also **KEERASSH** [Clint: The Hamster Triumphant #1, 1986] The crashing sound of breaking glass
KEERASSH see KEE-RASH
KEE-RUNCH [The Adventures of Bayou Billy #3, 1990] A crunching, hitting sound
KEKK [Dare Devil: The Man Without Fear vol.1 #2, 1993] The sound of a foot hitting and tripping over an object
KERAASH see KEE-RASH
KER-BASH [The Adventures of Bayou Billy #3, 1989] The sound made by crashing out a door
KER-PLASH [The Solution #5] A splashing sound
KER-SMASHH [The Adventures of Bayou Billy #3, 1990] A smashing sound, as that of breaking glass
KER-splash [Thunderstrike vol.1 #4, 1994] A large splashing sound, as that made by an object falling into water
KHAKK [Dare Devil: The Man Without Fear vol.1 #2, 1993] A cry of pain
KHRASSH [Dare Devil #194] The sound of breaking glass
KIDDO [Betty #40] A term of address directed to a person (usually) younger than oneself
KIFF [MAD #175, June 1975] The sound of a cough
KIKKI-TIKKI-KIKKI-TIKKI [MAD's Don Martin Cooks Up More Tales, 1976] The sound of an airplane motor quitting
KING KONG [Clint #1, 1986] The sound of bullets hitting armor

KIPUCKATA SPOP [MAD's Don Martin Cooks Up More Tales, 1976] The sounds of an airplane engine
KIT-TOONG [MAD's Don Martin Cooks Up More Tales, 1976] The sound of a falling person hitting the ground and then bouncing: also KITTOONG [MAD's Don Martin Cooks Up More Tales, 1976] The sound of a bounce
KITOONG see KIT-TOONG
KKKK [Captain Thunder and Blue Bolt #1] A crackling sound
K-K-KREAK [The Adventures of Bayou Billy #3, 1990] A creaking sound
KKKKRRRRRAAAAAKKKKKLLLL also KKKRAKKKLL [Captain Thunder and Blue Bolt #1] An electrical crackling sound: KKRAKL [Avengers West Coast Annual vol.2 #8, 1993] A crackling sound
KKKRAKKKLL see KKKKRRRRRAAAAAKKKKKLLLL
KKKRRRROOOMM [Captain Thunder and Blue Bolt #1] The sound of a roof caving in
KKKSH [MAD #244, January 1984] The sound made by a brick crashing through a window
KKKSSH [MAD's Don Martin Cooks Up More Tales, 1976] The sound of shattering glass
KKRAKL see KKKKRRRRRAAAAAKKKKKLLLL
K-KLAKT [Batman #502, 1993] The sound of an object hitting the floor
KKRITCH [Star Hunters vol.2 #5, 1978] A sound of weapon fire hitting rock
KLACK [The Adventures of Bayou Billy #4, 1990] The sound of a clip being inserted into an automatic weapon
KLAK [MAD's Don Martin Cooks Up More Tales, 1976] The sound of a boulder hitting the ground: [MAD #222, April 1981]: also KLICK [Dare Devil: The Man Without Fear vol.1 #3, 1993] The sound of a bolt moving in its lock
KLAKATA-KLAKATA [MAD's Don Martin Cooks Up More Tales, 1976] The sound of a conveyor belt in operation
KLANG [MAD #219, December 1980] The sound of a car collision: [MAD #238, April 1983] The sound of a radiator being hit with a hammer: [The Ren and Stimpy Show vol.1 #6, 1993] A figurative expression of sudden or instantaneous recovery
KLANGK [Avengers West Coast Annual vol.2 #8, 1993] The sound made by a kick
KLANK [Attack #41, 1983] A sound, as of a metal object hitting stone
KLANKT [Steel #1.1994] The clanking sound of metal
KLASHT [Batman #502, 1993] A crashing sound

KLICK see KLAKK
KLIK [MAD #216, July 1980] The sound of a hammer being cocked on a six gun: [MAD #222, April 1981] The sound of a lock being opened: [MAD #238, April 1983] The sound made by turning the channel knob on a TV: [Star Hunters vol.2 #5, 1978] The sound made by snapping fingers: [Batman #502, 1993] The clicking sound of a switch: [Prototype vol.1 #6, 1994] A mechanical sound, as of armor clicking shut: [The Night Man vol.1 #4, 1994] A sound made by a lever for a hidden entrance in a stone wall
KLIK-GROOON [MAD's Don Martin Cooks Up More Tales, 1976] The sound of a table fan being turned on and gaining speed
KLIKITA-KLKITA [MAD's Don Martin Cooks Up More Tales, 1976] The sound of a conveyor belt in operation
KLIK KLAK [MAD #177, September 1975] The sound of a bolt action: [MAD #233, September 1982] The sound of heels while walking
KLLIMP [The Ren and Stimpy Show vol.1 #6, 1993] A sound made by a person landing on a floor
KLINK [The Adventures of Captain Jack #7, 1987] "the KLINK" means "Jail"
KLINKADINK [MAD #252, January 1985] The sound of a coin being dropped into a coin operated machine
KLINK GLINK [MAD #202, December 1978] The sound of a coin being dropped into a coin operated machine
KLOMP [MAD #212, January 1980] The sound of a body hitting a wall
KLONK [MAD #218, October 1980] The sound of a body being hit by a car: [Clint: The Hamster Triumphant #1, 1986] The sound of a blow to the head; A kicking sound
KLONNK [Madballs vol.1 #7, 1987] The sound of a frozen body falling to the ground
KLOOM [MAD #218, October 1980] A sound made by kicking a door
KLOON [MAD's Don Martin Cooks Up More Tales, 1976] The sound of a huge wooden beam hitting the ground on it's end
KLOONK [MAD #181, March 1976] The sound of a person walking into a telephone pole
KLOOONN [MAD #222, April 1981] The sound of a metal door falling and squashing a person
KLOP [Madballs vol.1 #7, 1987] A sound as of a wooden mallet when used to knock the head off of a figurine

KLUD [Clint #1, 1986] The sound a falling body makes when it strikes the ground: [Dare Devil: The Man Without Fear vol.1 #3, 1993] A kicking sound: [2099 Unlimited vol.1 #2, 1993] A sound made by hitting a head with a heavy object
KLUDD [The Adventures of Bayou Billy #4, 1990] The thud-like sound of a face smashing into a wall: [NFL SuperPro vol.1 #9, 1992] A sound similar to a thud, as when a body hits against a wall: [2099 Unlimited vol.1 #3, 1993] A hitting sound: [2099 Unlimited vol.1 #2, 1993] The dull sound of a kick to the head
KLUGG [Dare Devil: The Man Without Fear vol.1 #4, 1994] A hitting sound
KLUNK [Son of MAD, 1973] The sound of a bottle being put on a table: [Detective Comics vol.47 #529, 1983] A sound made when objects strike one another: [The Adventures of Bayou Billy #3, 1990] A hitting sound: [Ralph Snart Adventures vol.5, 1993] The sound of an object hitting the floor
KNOCK [Ripley's Believe It Or Not: True Ghost Stories #53, 1975] A knocking sound, as of on a door: also KNOK [The Adventures of Bayou Billy #4, 1990] A knocking sound: also KNOK KNOCK [The Adventures of Bayou Billy #2, 1989] The sound of knocking on a door
KNOK see KNOCK
KNOK KNOCK see KNOCK
KOFF [Cold Blooded Chamelion Commando #1, 1986] The sound of a cough
KONK [Clint #1, 1986] A kicking sound: [Dare Devil: The Man Without Fear vol.1 #5, 1994] The sound made by the application of a Bo to the head
KPOW [The Solution vol.1 #2, 1993] The sound of gunfire
K-POW [Detective Comics vol.47 #529, 1983] The sound of an explosion
KRAAASH [Mantra vol.1 #7, 1994] A crashing sound
KRAACK see KRACK
KRA-ACK see KRACK
KRAAK see KRACK
KRACK also KRAACK also KRA-ACK [Superboy #154, 1969] A cracking sound: [The Solution vol.1 #2, 1993] A punching sound [Our Fighting Forces #111, 1968] also KRAAK [The Solution vol.1 #2, 1993] A punching sound: KRAK [MAD #181, March 1976] The sound of twigs being snapped: [MAD #211, December 1979] The sound of gunfire: [MAD #244, January 1984] The sound of a punch: [Captain Marvel vol.1 #42, 1976] The sound of a body hitting a wall:

[Attack #41, 1983] The sound of a gunshot: [Avengers West Coast Annual vol.2 #8, 1993] The sound of a club applied to a head: [Dare Devil: The Man Without Fear vol.1 #5, 1994] The sound of a door being kicked open: [The Adventures of Bayou Billy #4, 1990] A punching sound: [Clint #1, 1986] The sound of heads knocking together: [Batman #502, 1993] The sound of electronic weapon fire: also KRAKC [NFL SuperPro vol.1 #9, 1992] A cracking sound: [2099 Unlimited vol.1 #2, 1993] A sound made when crashing into plate glass

KRACK KRACK [The Adventures of Bayou Billy #2, 1989] The sound of automatic gunfire

KRACKLE [The Adventures of Bayou Billy #2, 1989] The sound of a flame thrower

KRA DA BOOM [Hawkeye vol.2 #3, 1994] The sound of an explosion

KRAGSH [2099 Unlimited vol.1 #2, 1993] A sound made when crashing into plate glass

KRAK see KRACK

KRAKA DOOM [Darkhold: Pages From The Book of Sins vol.1 #7, 1993] The sound of an energy bolt

KRAKADOOM [War Machine vol.1 #1, 1994] The sound of an explosion

KRAKATOWWW [War Machine vol.1 #1, 1994] The sound of an explosion

KRAKC see KRACK

KRAKCH see KRACK

KRAKK [The Solution #5] The sound of knuckles cracking: [NFL SuperPro vol.1 #9, 1992] A hitting sound: [Dare Devil: The Man Without Fear vol.1 #2, 1993] A breaking sound, as achieved by a kick to the knee: [Dare Devil: The Man Without Fear vol.1 #4, 1993] A sound made by striking sharply with a bo

KRAKKL also **KRAKKKL** also **KRAKKLL** [Captain Thunder and Blue Bolt #1] An electric crackling sound

KRAKKKL see KRAKKL

KRAKKLL see KRAKKL

KRAKKLE [Star Hunters vol.2 #5, 1978] The sound made by a force field

KRAKOOOOM [The Solution vol.1 #2, 1994] The sound of an explosion

KRAKOW [The Anomalies #1, 2000] A sound of electronic weapon fire

KRAM [The Vision and The Scarlet Witch vol.2 #7, 1986] A punching sound

KRANCH [Venom: Lethal Protector #3, 1993] A crunching sound, as when vehicles collide

KRARASH [Star Hunters vol.2 #5, 1978] A crashing sound, as of a collision

KRASH [MAD #188, January 1977] The sound of a boulder crashing to earth: [Darkhold: Pages From The Book of Sins vol.1 #7, 1993] also K-RASH [Clint: The Hamster Triumphant #1, 1986] A crashing sound: [Captain Justice #1] The sound of a breaking wall: [Mantra: Infinity, 1995] The sound of breaking glass

KRASHH [The Adventures of Bayou Billy #3, 1990] The sound of breaking glass

KRA TAKKA TAKKA TAKKA TAM [2099 Unlimited vol.1 #4, 1993] The crumbling sounds of a falling wall

KRA-THAM [The Incredible Hulk vol.1 #226, 1978] A smashing or breaking sound

KRA-TINKLE [The Adventures of Bayou Billy #4, 1990] The sound of breaking glass

KREEE [Dare Devil: The Man Without Fear vol.1 #4, 1994] The sound made when a board that is nailed down is pulled or pried away

KREEK [MAD #232, July 1982] The sound of a clothesline pulley

KREESH [Venom: Lethal Protector #3, 1993] A punching sound

KRESH [Clint #1, 1986] A kicking sound

KRESHH [Dare Devil: The Man Without Fear vol.1 #2, 1993] A crashing sound, as of breaking glass

KRISSH [Mantra vol.1 #2, 1993] The sound of smashing glass

KRIZZ [The Adventures of Bayou Billy #2, 1989] The sound of a flame thrower

KRNCH [Dare Devil: The Man Without Fear vol.1 #5, 1994] A crunching sound, as of a collision

KROOM [2099 Unlimited vol.1 #3, 1993] The sound of an explosion

KROOOM [Steel #1.1994] A hitting sound, as with a cast iron frying pan

KROOOOOSHHH [The Adventures of Bayou Billy #2, 1989] The sound of a flame thrower

KRRAAASSSHH [Ultraman vol.1 #1, 1994] A crashing sound, as of breaking glass

KRRAKKLLL [Captain Thunder and Blue Bolt #1] The sound made by a bolt of electricity

KRRIK [The Solution #5] The sound of knuckles cracking

KRRKK [Unlimited vol.1 #2, 1993] A cracking sound

KRRUMP [Detective Comics vol.47 #529, 1983] The sound of someone falling on their keester

KR-RUNCH [Superboy #154, 1969] A crunching sound
KRUKK [Dare Devil: The Man Without Fear vol.1 #2, 1993] A kicking sound
KRUMP [Dare Devil: The Man Without Fear vol.1 #5, 1994] The sound of a security screen in a police cruiser being kicked out
KRUNCH KRINKLE KRINKLE KRITCH [MAD #221, March 1981] The sounds made by crushing tinfoil into a ball
KRUNK [MAD #225, September 1981] The sound made when attempting to eat a popcorn seed: [Steel #1.1994] The crunching sound of metal
KRUNTCH [Avengers West Coast Annual vol.2 #8, 1993] The sound of a body hitting a wall
KRUUK [Captain Thunder and Blue Bolt #1] The sound of rock falling down a mountainside
KSSHFWOOM [MAD #230, April 1982] The sound of a skydiver landing with a defective parachute
KSSSH see KSSSHHHH
KSSSHHHH [Cold Blooded Chamelion Commando #1, 1986] also KSSSH [2099 Unlimited vol.1 #2, 1993] The crashing sound of breaking glass
KTAAASHHH [Thunderstrike vol.1 #4, 1994] A crashing sound, as of breaking glass
KTAK [Clint #1, 1986] The sound of an object breaking
KTAK KTAK BALOWM [Son of MAD, 1973] The sound of multiple lightning strikes and thunder
KTANGG [Dare Devil: The Man Without Fear vol.1 #2, 1993] The sound of vibrating metal
KTHUMP [Superboy #154, 1969] A thumping sound, as when a rock is thrown at a dog; The sound of a heartbeat
KTHUNK [Superboy #154, 1969] The sound of a collision
KTOW [Son of MAD, 1973] The sound of a gunshot
KUD [Clint #1, 1986] also KUDD [Dare Devil: The Man Without Fear vol.1 #4, 1994] A kicking sound
KUDD see KUD
KUGG [Dare Devil: The Man Without Fear vol.1 #2, 1993] A punching sound
KUH-WANG [Avengers West Coast Annual vol.2 #8, 1993] A punching sound
KUKK [Dare Devil: The Man Without Fear vol.1 #3, 1993] The sound of a knee to a jaw; A kicking sound; [Dare Devil: The Man Without Fear vol.1 #4, 1994] The sound of a locker door being kicked in: [Dare Devil: The Man Without Fear vol.1 #5, 1994] The sound of a Bo applied to a head

KUMP [Dare Devil: The Man Without Fear vol.1 #2, 1993] The sound of a collision
KUNK [Dare Devil: The Man Without Fear vol.1 #4, 1994] The sound of a Bo applied to a body
KU-RONNCH [2099 Unlimited vol.1 #3, 1993] A loud crunching sound
KWAM [The Punisher: War Zone vol.1 #1, 1993] The sound of a collision: also KWAMM [The Adventures of Bob Hope #95, 1965] The sound made by a stomach punch
KWAMM see KWAM
KWONG [MAD #214, April 1980] The sound you'd hear if you got a wrecking ball in the face
KWOOOOMP [Venom: Lethal Protector #3, 1993] The sound of weapon fire hitting a truck
KWUFF [Thunderstrike vol.1 #4, 1994] The sound of a body being slammed into a wall
KZAKK [The Solution #8] The sound of a blast from an electronic weapon
KZAT also KZZZAT [Star Hunters vol.2 #5, 1978] The sound of electronic weapon fire
KZZZAT see KZAT
LEBOOM [MAD #252, January 1985] The sound of an explosion in French
MABBIT [MAD #233, September 1982] The sound of bodies in collision
MEOROWWWGHHH also Meorowwwgssh [Clint: The Hamster Triumphant #1, 1986] A cat's meow
Meorowwwgssh see MEOROWWWGHHH
MFFFF... [X-Factor vol.1 #84, 1992] A kissing sound
MMM [Superboy #154, 1969] also MMMM [The Adventures of Captain Jack #7, 1987] A sound that signifies that a thought process is in progress
MMM also MMMMMMM [The Adventures of Captain Jack #7, 1987] also MMMMM also MMMMMM [The Ren and Stimpy Show vol.1 #6, 1993] A sound expressing enjoyment, as of food
MMMBUH-WHAMMM [The Adventures of Bayou Billy #2, 1989] The complex sound of a monster truck crashing through a wall
Mmm-Hmm [MAD's Don Martin Cooks Up More Tales, 1976] The sound of humming
MMMM see MMM
Mmmm hmmm [MAD #230, April 1982] Means "Yes"
MMMMM see MMM
MMMMMM see MMMMM

MMMMMMM see MMM

MMMMMMMM [The Adventures of Bayou Billy #2, 1989] A kissing sound

MMMMMMMMMMMMMMM [X-Factor vol.1 #84, 1992] A kissing sound

MMMOOOOO [Son of MAD, 1973] The sound of an angry bull

MMMMPH [The Adventures of Captain Jack #7, 1987] A sound expressing enjoyment

MMMPPPHHHHH also **MMMWWWAAA** also **MMMWWWUUHH** [The Ren and Stimpy Show vol.1 #6, 1993] A sound made by a person straining physically

MMMWWWAAA see MMMPPPHHHHH

MMMWWWUUHH see MMMPPPHHHHH

MOWM [MAD #238, April 1983] The sound of an atomic blast

MRFLLRB [Madballs vol.1 #7, 1987] Translation "Don't tread on me"

MUNCH [Cold Blooded Chamelion Commando #1, 1986] An eating sound

MVS BBBL KURRRTZ [Madballs vol.1 #7, 1987] Translation "We Came, We Saw, We Madballed!!"

NAAAAA [2099 Unlimited vol.1 #4, 1993] A cry of pain

NAAAAH see NAAAH

NAAAH also **NAAAAH** [The Twisted Tantrum of the Purple Snit #1, 1980] A word meaning "No"

NAW [The Adventures of Captain Jack #7, 1987] Means "No"

NFF [Dare Devil: The Man Without Fear vol.1 #2, 1993] The sound of a grunt

NNGHHH [The Ren and Stimpy Show vol.1 #6, 1993] A sound made by a person straining physically

NNN NNN [Hawkeye vol.2 #3, 1994] A soft sound made while sleeping or dreaming

NNNNNNNG [Mantra vol.1 #7, 1994] An utterance of pain

NOK [Dare Devil #194] A knocking sound: NOKK [Avengers West Coast Annual vol.2 #8, 1993] A knocking sound, as of a club to the head: NOK NOK [Mantra vol.1 #2, 1993] The sound of a door knock

NOKK see NOK

NOK NOK see NOK

NOOOO [Lethal Foes of Spiderman vol.1 #4, 1993] also **NOOOOOO** [G.I.Joe vol.1 #104, 1990] also **NO-O-O-O-O** [The Adventures of Bayou Billy #2, 1989] A prolonged "No"; A cry of protest or disagreement

NO-O-O-O-O see NOOOO

NOOOOOO see NOOOO

NYAH [Betty #40] A child's word, usually repeated, used to taunt and tease another

NYA HA HA [The Adventures of Toucan Sam, 1994] The sound of an evil laugh

Nyak...Gniff...unk [MAD Super Special 16, 1975] Sounds made by a monster

NYARGH [The Adventures of Bayou Billy #3, 1990] A snarling animal sound

NYARL also NYARRL also NYRL [The Adventures of Bayou Billy #3, 1990] A snarling animal sound

NYARRL see NYARL

NYRL see NYARL

OH [The Adventures of Captain Jack #7, 1987] A sound of enjoyment

OHH [Bobby Sherman #6, 1972] An exclamation of surprise

OH-OH [Bobby Sherman #6, 1972] An exclamation indicating that something is wrong

OMIGOD [Cold Blooded Chamelion Commando #1, 1986] Means "Oh My God!", a mildly blasphemous expression of surprise, wonderment etc

OOF [MAD #221, March 1981] A sound made during lovemaking: also OOOOF [Betty #40] The noise made by a person when they have the wind knocked out of them: [Dare Devil: The Man Without Fear vol.1 #3, 1993] An exclamation of pain, as when struck: OOFPH [Avengers West Coast Annual vol.2 #8, 1993] A cry of pain

OOFPH see OOF

oohhhhh [The Adventures of Bayou Billy #2, 1989] A moaning sound

OOO also OOOH [MAD #177, September 1975]: also OOOOO also OOOOOO [The Adventures of Captain Jack #7, 1987] also OOOO [Betty #40] An exclamation or interjection of surprise, enjoyment, excitement, pleasure, disappointment, upset, admiration etc: An interjection expressing the occurrence of a sudden bright idea: [The Punisher: War Zone vol.1 #1, 1993] The sound of a train horn: OOOOO [Betty #40] A cooing sound of love, affection etc: an interjection expressing excitement: OOOOOO [The Twisted Tantrum of the Purple Snit #1, 1980] The sound of moaning; also OOOOOOO [Betty #40] The sound of crying; A cooing sound expressing admiration, love etc; An interjection expressing disappointment: also OOO...OOO...OO [Betty #40, 1996] A sound signifying worry, upset etc

OOOH see OOO

OOOO see OOO
OOOOF see OOF
OOOOO see OOO
OOOOOO see OOO
OOOOOOO see OOO
OOO...OOO...OO see OOO
OO-OOPS see OOOPS
Ooooops... see OOOPS
OOOOPS see OOOPS
OOOPS [Betty #40] also OO-OOPS [New Kids On The Block: Magic Summer Tour, 1990] also Ooooops... [MAD #212, January 1980] also OOOOPS [MAD #227, December 1981] also OOOPS [MAD #181, March 1976] A sound made to indicate an error or blunder has occurred
OOOSSH [Madballs vol.1 #7, 1987] The sound of a rocket in flight
OOOUUUCHHH [The Twisted Tantrum of the Purple Snit #1, 1980] A cry of pain
OOWW [New Kids On The Block: Step By Step, 1990] The sound of a dog baying
OOWW see OW
ORG [The Adventures of Captain Jack #7, 1987] A gulping sound
OUCH [Mantra vol.1 #5, 1993] An utterance of pain
OUTTA [Mantra vol.1 #5, 1993] Means "Out of"
OW [The Adventures of Tintin: Explorers on the Moon, 1954] also OOWW [2099 Unlimited vol.1 #4, 1993] also OWW [Ripley's Believe It Or Not: True Ghost Stories #53, 1975] also OWWW [X-Factor vol.1 #84, 1992] also OWWWW [Avengers West Coast Annual vol.2 #8, 1993] also OWWWWWW [MAD #212, January 1980] A cry of pain
OWOOO [Superboy #154, 1969] A dog yelp
OWW see OW
OWWW see OW
OWWWW see OW
OWWWWWWW see OW
PADAP [MAD #249, September 1984] The sound of a running footstep
PAF [MAD #177, September 1975] The sound of a magical change, as in a frog to a prince: [MAD #215, June 1980] The sound of an explosion
PAFF [Lucky Luke: Canyon Apache, 1971] The sound of a punch to the face
PAH [The Punisher: War Zone vol.1#1,1993] The sound of a bullet hitting stone

PAN [Lucky Luke: Canyon Apache, 1971] The sound of gunfire
PANG [The Twisted Tantrum of the Purple Snit #1, 1980] The sound of a ricochet
PAROOM [Star Hunters vol.2 #4, 1978] The sound of an explosion
PCHOOM [2099 Unlimited vol.1 #2, 1993] The sound of an explosion
PEK [MAD #221, March 1981] The sound of a single ball bounce
PEK PEK PEK [MAD #221, March 1981] The sound of a bouncing ball
PFFFT [MAD #222, April 1981] The sound of a paint can being sprayed
PFFHT [War Machine vol.1 #1, 1994] The sound of a heat seeking missile being deployed
PHAK [The Adventures of Bayou Billy #4, 1990] A punching sound
PHEW [The Adventures of Kool-Aid Man #6, 1989] A sigh of relief
PHFFFTT see PHFFT
PHFFT also PHFFFTT [The Adventures of Bayou Billy #2, 1989] The sound of a blowpipe
PHFISSHT [The Adventures of Bayou Billy #2, 1989] The sound of an oxy-acetylene gas welder
PHHHHHT also PHHHHHT [G.I.Joe vol.1 #104, 1990] The sound of a dart in flight
PHHHHHT see PHHHHHHT
PHOOK [Dead Pool: The Circle Chase #4, 1993] A punching sound
PHOONT [Dead Pool: The Circle Chase #4, 1993] The sound of a weapon shot
PHooo [MAD #181, March 1976] A blowing sound
PHROOOM [Avengers West Coast Annual vol.2 #8, 1993] The sound of an explosion
PH-SHOOSH [The Adventures of Bayou Billy #2, 1989] The sound of a flame thrower
PHTOOP [Crackbusters #1, 1986] The sound made by punching someone in the mouth
PHTOW [Avengers West Coast Annual vol.2 #8, 1993] A hitting sound
PIK PIK PIK [MAD #216, July 1980] The sound made by chipping into wood
PING [Our Fighting Forces #111, 1968] The sound of a ricochet: [Cold Blooded Chamelion Commando #1, 1986] The

sound of a bullet in flight: [Cold Blooded Chamelion Commando #1, 1986] The sound of an elevator floor indicator
PING PANG [Clint #1, 1986] The sound of bullets hitting armor
PITOOIE [MAD #217, September 1980] A spitting sound
PITTER-PAT [The Adventures of Bayou Billy #3, 1989] The sound of running footsteps
PIUNG [The Twisted Tantrum of the Purple Snit #1, 1980] The sound of a ricochet
PLAFF [Lucky Luke: Canyon Apache, 1971] A punching sound
PLASH [2099 Unlimited vol.1 #3, 1993] A splashing sound
PLEEP [Star Hunters vol.2 #5, 1978] The sound of shields going up
PLIC-K [MAD #232, July 1982] The sound of electricity being turned off
PLIK [Son of MAD, 1973] The sound of a sling shot being fired
PLINK [MAD #246, April 1984] The sound of a coin hitting the ground: [Venom: The Enemy Within vol.1 #1, 1994] The sound of a breaking beer glass: also plink [MAD #246, April 1984] The sound heard from a distance of a coin hitting the ground
plink see PLINK
PLIP [Star Hunters vol.2 #4, 1978] The sound of armament banks freezing up: [Venom: Lethal Protector #3, 1993] also PLIPPPP [Venom: The Enemy Within #2, 1994] The sound of a wrist web being deployed
PLIPPLE [MAD #233, September 1982] The sound of soup
PLIPPPP see PLIP
PLOBBLE [MAD #233, September 1982] The sound of soup
PLOIPLE also PLOPLE [MAD's Don Martin Cooks Up More Tales, 1976] The sound of a tear falling into a puddle of tears
PLOK [Son of MAD, 1973] The sound of a sling shot being fired
PLOOPPLOOPPLOOP [Mantra vol.1 #7, 1994] A dripping sound
PLOP [MAD #177, September 1975] The sound of a hat falling to the ground: [Bobby Sherman #6, 1972] A slopping sound: [Madballs vol.1 #2, 1987] The sound of toxic waste percolating in a chemical pond
PLOPLE see PLOIPLE
PLORF [MAD #211, December 1979] The sound of food being flung from a fork

PLORK [MAD #211, December 1979] The sound of a mother bird feeding her young
PLORP [2099 Unlimited vol.1 #3, 1993] A splashing sound
PLORTCH [MAD #227, December 1981] The sound of a sword blade stabbing into a body
PLOUF [Lucky Luke: Canyon Apache, 1971] A diving sound
PLOW [The Vision and The Scarlet Witch vol.2 #7, 1986] A hitting sound
PLUNK [MAD #221, March 1981] The sound of an object landing in a trash can: [Detective Comics vol.47 #529, 1983] The sound made a stone lobbed into water
PLURP [The Adventures of Bayou Billy #4, 1990] Bubble sounds as those made when a head is held under water involuntarily
POING [MAD #215, June 1980] The sound of a spring loaded flare gun
POINK [Venom: Lethal Protector #3, 1993] A bouncing sound, as of a sonic grenade bouncing on a sidewalk: [Ralph Snart Adventures #5, 1993] The sound of a limb being torn off: [Avengers West Coast Annual vol.2, #8 1993] The sound of a small metallic hit, as of a pebble bouncing off armor
POIT [The Ren and Stimpy Show vol.1 #6, 1993] The sound of a lid popping off a can
POK [MAD's Don Martin Cooks Up More Tales, 1976] The sound of a body thrown from a height and hitting the ground: [Clint #1, 1986] A hitting sound; [Batman #502, 1993] The sound of a bullet hitting an object
PONG [MAD's Don Martin Cooks Up More Tales, 1976] The sound of a lead pipe hitting an object
POOF [Crackbusters #1, 1986] A magical sound usually heard when a somethingness goes into, or comes out of, a nothingness, as when a leprechaun suddenly appears: [MAD #175, June 1975] The sound of a magical transformation, as of a frog to a princess: [MAD #209, September 1979] The sound of a fire starting
POOM also POOMF also POOMP [Star Hunters vol.2 #4, 1978] The sound of explosive clamps discharging: [2099 Unlimited vol.1 #2, 1993] The sound of an explosion: [FREEX #7, 1994] The sound of bullets hitting a road: [Wonderman #12, 1992] A punching sound: [2099 Unlimited vol.1 #2, 1993] The sound of gunfire
POOMF see POOM
POOMP see POOM
POOOFT [Mantra vol.1 #5, 1993] A sound accompanying a vanishment

POOOOOF [The Adventures of Bayou Billy #3, 1989] The sound of an exploding smoke bomb
POP [Son of MAD, 1973] The sound of an inflated membrane exploding: [The Adventures of Kool-Aid Man #6, 1989] The sound occasionally heard upon the materialization of a magic doorway: [Dead Pool: The Circle Chase #4, 1993] A popping sound, as of mechanical parts coming undone: [Dare Devil: The Man Without Fear vol.1 #4, 1994] The sound of a bubblegum bubble breaking: [The Anomalies #1, 2000] A hitting sound
POPPA POPPA-BOP [The Adventures of Bayou Billy #2, 1989] The sound of automatic gunfire
POT [Captain Marvel vol.1 #42, 1976] The sound of a gun being knocked out of a hand
POW [Our Fighting Forces #111, 1968] The sound of gunfire: [Captain Marvel vol.1 #42, 1976] A punching sound
POWW [Detective Comics vol.47 #529, 1983] The sound of an exploding spray canister
PPRRRR [Catwoman #6, 1994] The purring sound of a cat
PRAYKKK [Avengers West Coast Annual vol.2 #8, 1993] A raking, slashing sound as one made with claws
PRUKT [Batman #502, 1993] A mechanical sound, as would be made by a weapon and a metallic holster
PRZZAT [Star Hunters vol.2 #4, 1978] A sound of electronic weapon fire
PSSSH [MAD Super Special Number 31, Summer 1980] The sound made by a spray can
PTAK [2099 Unlimited vol.1 #2, 1993] The sound of gunfire hitting the ground
PTANG [The Adventures of Bayou Billy #4, 1990] The sound of a bullet hitting the ground
P-TANG [Clint #1, 1986] The sound of a bullet hitting armor
PTHOOOM [Avengers West Coast Annual vol.2 #8, 1993] The sound of an explosion
PTHUMP [The Adventures of Bayou Billy #3, 1990] A hitting sound
PTOK [The Adventures of Bayou Billy #4, 1990] A punching sound
PTOO [Son of MAD, 1973] A spitting sound
PTOOEY [The Adventures of Bob Hope #95, 1965] The sound of a giant vacuum spitting villains into a public waste can
PTOOM [Captain Thunder and Blue Bolt #1] An explosive sound, as that of an object struck by a bolt of electricity
PTOW [Captain Marvel vol.1 #42, 1976] A punching sound

PUFF, PUFF [Son of MAD, 1973] The sound of a person out of breath
PUNCH [G.I.Joe vol.1 #61, 1987] The sound of a gunshot
PWAKA-PWOOM [The Solution #5] The sound of an explosion
PWEE [2099 Unlimited vol.1 #3, 1993] The sound of a bullet in flight
PWOOM [2099 Unlimited vol.1 #2, 1993] A sound made when a body smashes into a wall
QUACK WAAK WAAK [MAD Super Special 16, 1975] The quacking sounds of a duck
RAAARR [X-Factor vol.1 #84, 1992] A roar
RAH [MAD #227, December 1981] A cheer
RAKKKT [Mantra vol.1 #7, 1994] A breaking sound, as of a vehicle crashing through a wooden barrier
RAP [Madballs vol.1 #7, 1987] A mechanical knocking sound
RAPRAPRAP [MAD #252, January 1985] The sound of a cup being hit on a counter
RATATAT [Our Fighting Forces #111, 1968] also RATATATAT also RATATATA also RATATATATAT also RATATATATATA [MAD #177, September 1975] also RATATATATATAT also RATATATATATATA [Fightin' Marines #145, 1979] also RAT-TA-TA-TA also RAT-TA-TAT also RAT-TAT also RAT-TAT-TAT [Attack #41, 1983] also RATA-TATTATTATTAT [Cold Blooded Chamelion Commando #1, 1986] also RATATATATATATAT [G.I.Joe vol.1 #104, 1990] The sound of a machine gun
RATATATAT see RATATAT
RATATATATA see RATATAT
RATATATATAT see RATATAT
RATATATATATA see RATATAT
RATA..TATA..TA..TA [MAD #241, September 1983] The sound of a pneumatic drill
RATATATATATAT see RATATAT
RATATATATATATA see RATATAT
RATATATATATATAT see RATATAT
RATA-TATTATTATTAT see RATATAT
RAT-TAT see RATATAT
RAT-TA-TAT see RATATAT
RAT-TA-TA-TA see RATATAT
RAT-TAT-TAT see RATATAT
RATTATATTAT [MAD #222, April 1981] The sound of a drum roll
RAUGHHHHHH [Venom: The Enemy Within #2, 1994] The roaring sound of a sonic blast

REEEE [Mantra vol.1 #7, 1994] A cry of pain
REEEEEEE [Star Wars Vol.1 #6 1977] The sound of an alarm
RIBBIT [MAD #232, July 1982] The sound of a frog's croak
RIIPP see RIP
RING [The Adventures of Captain Jack #7, 1987] also RINNG also RIN-NG also R-RING [New Kids On The Block: Step By Step, 1990] also RING-A-LING [Son of MAD, 1973] also RRING also RRRINNG [Bobby Sherman #6, 1972] The sound of a telephone ringer: RRRING also RRRRING [The Adventures of Tintin: Explorers on the Moon, 1954] A ringing sound: also RRRRIINNNNGGG [Detective Comics vol.47 #529, 1983] The sound of an alarm
RINK-RIK [The Adventures of Bayou Billy #4, 1990] The sound of windshield wipers
RINNG see RING
RIN-NG see RING
RIP [Ralph Snart Adventures #5, 1993] also RIPP [MAD #225, September 1981] also RRIPP also RRRIPP [The Night Man vol.1 #4, 1994] also RRRIP [Clint: The Hamster Triumphant #1, 1986] also RIP-PP-P-P [The Adventures of Bayou Billy #3, 1990] also RRRRIIIIPPP [The Adventures of Toucan Sam, 1994] A ripping, tearing sound: RIIPP [Prototype vol.1 #6, 1994] A ripping sound, as of a panel being torn off
RIP-PP-P-P see RIP
ROARARL see ROARRRR
ROARL see ROARRRR
ROARRRR [G.I.Joe vol.1 #61, 1987] A roaring sound, as of a truck engine: also ROARARL [The Adventures of Bayou Billy #3, 1990] also ROOOOR [2099 Unlimited vol.1 #3, 1993] also RRARR [Steel #1.1994] A roaring sound: also ROARL [The Adventures of Bayou Billy #3, 1990] A roaring animal sound: also RROARR [Madballs vol.1 #7, 1987] The sound of a stomach growling: also RROOAAARR [Pitt #1, 1993] A roaring sound, as of a motorcycle engine: also RRRAAARRRR also RRRRRRR [2099 Unlimited vol.1 #4, 1993] A roar of defiance, rage etc
ROLL [Archie #407, 1993] The sound made by a rolling object
ROOOOR see ROARRRR
ROWF also ROWFF [Superboy #154, 1969] The sound of a dog's bark
ROWFF see ROWF
ROWRR [Dare Devil: The Man Without Fear vol.1 #3, 1993] The sound of a dog bark

ROWRRR [MAD #223, June 1981] An unspecified TV sound
RRARR see ROARRRR
RRGL [FREEX #7, 1994] A gurgling sound, as made by a person whose throat has been torn out
RRING see RING
R-RING see RING
RRIPP see RIP
RROARR see ROARRRR
RROOAAARR see ROARRRR
RROWF [Son of MAD, 1973] A barking sound
RRRAAARRRR see ROARRRR
RRREEEEEEE [Venom: Lethal Protector #3, 1993] The sound of a scream
RRRG [Mantra vol.1 #7, 1994] A growling sound
RRRING see RING
RRRINNG see RING
RRRIP see RIP
RRRIPP see RIP
RRRRIIIIPPP see RIP
RRRMMMBBLLL [Avengers West Coast Annual vol.2 #8, 1993] A rolling, rumbling sound
RRR-OOOOOSHH [The Adventures of Bayou Billy #2, 1989] The sound of a flame thrower
R-RRR also **R-R-R-R** also **R-R-R-R-R** [Superboy #154, 1969] The sound of a dog's growl
R-R-R-R see R-RRR
RRRRAAAAAAA [The Ren and Stimpy Show vol.1 #6, 1993] A sound made by a person straining physically
RRRRAARGH [ROM #34, 1982] The roar of a sea serpent
RRRRHUUUMMM [The Adventures of Bayou Billy #2, 1989] The sound of a monster truck engine; The sound of a tank engine
RRRRIINNNNGGGG see RING
RRRRING see RING
RRRRR [MAD #229, March 1982] The sound of motorcycle engines
R-R-R-R-R see R-RRR
RRRRRR [MAD Super Special Number 31, Summer 1980] The sound of an ambulance siren
RRRRRRR see ROARRRR
RRRRRRRRMMMMMMMMMBBLL see RRRUMMMMBLLE
RRRRRRRRRRRRRRRROOOOSSSHH [Captain Thunder and Blue Bolt #1] The sound of an avalanche

RRRUMMMMBLLE [Darkhold: Pages from the Book of Sins vol.1 #7, 1993] also **RRRUMMBLLE** [Cold Blooded Chamelion Commando #1, 1986] also **RRRRRRRMMMMMMMMMBBLL** [Captain Thunder and Blue Bolt #1] also **RUMMMMMM** [Captain Justice #1] A prolonged rumbling sound
RRRUMMBLLE see **RRRUMMMMBLLE**
RR-UFF [Superboy #154, 1969] The sound of a dog's bark
RRUNCHT [Batman #502, 1993] A crunching, crashing sound
RRZZTTT [Star Hunters vol.2 #4, 1978] The sound of electronic weapon fire
RUB-A-DUB DUB-A-DUB A-DUB [Monkey Shines of Marseleen, 1906] The sound of a drum
RUMBLE [MAD's Don Martin Cooks Up More Tales, 1976] The sound of a volcano beginning to erupt: [MAD #188, January 1977] The sound of a boulder rolling down a mountain: [The Adventures of Captain Jack #7, 1987] A rumbling sound
RUMMMMMM see **RRRUMMMMBLLE**
RYENK [Cable #5, 1993] The sound of a panel being torn off
SCARF [The Ren and Stimpy Show vol.1 #6, 1993] An eating sound
SCHLIKT [Wolverine #75] The extruding sound of Wolverine's claws
SCHLLICKKK [Venom: The Enemy Within vol.1 #1, 1994] A sound made by stabbing with a bladed weapon
SCHPLOOK [Dead Pool: The Circle Chase #4, 1993] A sound made by a rapidly extending mechanical arm
SCHWOK [Batman #502, 1993] The sound made by a kick to the head
SCRATCH SCRATCH [The Adventures of Bayou Billy #2, 1989] The sound of someone scratching
SCREAM [MAD #177, September 1975] The sound of people screaming on a roller coaster
SCREECH also **SCREEECH** [Dare Devil: The Man Without Fear vol.1 #2, 1993] also **SCREEE** [Star Hunters vol.2 #5, 1978] also **SCREEEE** [Star Hunters vol.2 #5, 1978] also **SCREEEEE** [Detective Comics vol.47 #529, 1983] also **SCREEEEEEECHH** [FREEX #7, 1994] also **SKEEEE** also **SKEEEEE** [Dare Devil #277] also **SKREEE** [Venom: Lethal Protector #3, 1993] also **SKREEEE** [G.I.Joe vol.1 #61, 1987] also **SKREEEEEEEE** [The Punisher: War Zone vol.1 #1, 1993] also **SKREEL** [Ralph Snart Adventures #5, 1993] also **SCREEECHHH** [Archie #407, 1993] also **SCREEEECCHH** [The Adventures of Bayou Billy #4, 1990] The screeching

sound, as sometimes made by tires: also SCREEECH [Archie #407, 1993] A scream or cry of terror
SCREEECH see SCREECH
SCREEECHHH see SCREECH
SCREEEE see SCREECH
SCREEEECCHH see SCREECH
SCREEEEE see SCREECH
SCREEEEEE [Venom: The Enemy Within #2, 1994] A scream: [Steel #1.1994] The sound of squealing tires
SCREEEEEECHH see SCREECH
SCREEEEK [Mantra vol.1 #7, 1994] A breaking sound
SCRNCH [Pitt #1, 1993] A crunching sound, as of a body part being injured
SFROOSH [ROM #37, 1982] The sound of Plasmifire (similar in nature to napalm)
SHAAKKOW [Darkhold #10, 1993] The sound of an explosion
SHA-BLAM [2099 Unlimited vol.1 #4, 1993] A hitting sound
SHADDAP [Cold Blooded Chamelion Commando #1, 1986] Means "Shut up"
SHAK [NFL SuperPro vol.1 #9, 1992] A hitting sound: [2099 Unlimited vol.1 #4, 1993] The sound of electronic weapon fire
SHAKITYSHAKESHAKE [The Ren and Stimpy Show vol.1 #6, 1993] A sound made by something being shaken, as of a salt shaker
SHAKKKT [Mantra vol.1 #7, 1994] A bladed weapon cutting sound
ShaKOOM [Prototype vol.1 #6, 1994] The sound of an explosion
SHARAK [2099 Unlimited vol.1 #4, 1993] The sound of flying debris hitting an object
SHA-ZAM [The Twisted Tantrum of the Purple Snit #1, 1980] A magical word
SHAZ...HIC [MAD #177, September 1975] The sound of a magical incantation interrupted by a hiccough
SHAZZAP [The Anomalies #1, 2000] A sound of electronic weapon fire
SHAZZATZ [MAD #229, March 1982] A sweeping sound
SHCHUKK [ROM #35, 1982] A sound made when slammed and pinned to a wall with a trident
SHFFF [Detective Comics vol.47 #529, 1983] A sound made by an object being moved smoothly
SHH-FOOM [The Adventures of Bayou Billy #3, 1989] The sound of an exploding mustard gas canister
SHHHHH [Maxx #5, 1993] A hushing sound made to quieten someone

SHIIIIIIING [Thunderstrike vol.1 #2, 1994] The ringing sound of a mace hitting a helmet
SHIK [MAD's Don Martin Cooks Up More Tales, 1976] The sound of a plate moved across a floor
SHIKA [MAD's Don Martin Cooks Up More Tales, 1976] The sound of a package being shaken
SHIKA-SHIKA [MAD #217, September 1980] The sound of flint being rubbed to make sparks for fire
SHING [Batman #502, 1993] The ringing sound of a bladed weapon in flight
SHKILITZ [MAD #231, June 1982] The sound of surgery
SHKLAP [MAD's Don Martin Cooks Up More Tales, 1976] The sound of water being squirted
SHKLIZORTCH [MAD #231, June 1982] The sound of a spray of water to the face
SHKLOORT [MAD #229, March 1982] The sound of a sculptor working with clay
SHKREEUUHHHH [2099 Unlimited vol.1 #3, 1993] The peculiar sound of metal giving way under stress
SHKSHH [Dare Devil: The Man Without Fear vol.1 #3, 1993] A sound made as a person swims under water
SHK-SHKT [Pitt #1, 1993] The sound of a pump action on a shotgun
SHLIPP [MAD #233, September 1982] The sound of soup
SHLOMP [G.I.Joe vol.1 #104, 1990] The sound a body makes when hitting the ground, perhaps having fallen out of a window
SHLOOP [MAD #233, September 1982] The sound of soup
SHLORP [Darkhold #10, 1993] A dripping, slurping sound
SHLURP [MAD #233, September 1982] The sound of soup
SHMAMP [MAD #244, January 1984] A hitting sound
Shoo-be-doo [MAD's Don Martin Cooks Up More Tales, 1976] Musical sounds
shoo-boo...dah-be-dah [MAD's Don Martin Cooks Up More Tales, 1976] Musical sounds
SHOOKA SHOOKA SHOOKA [MAD #223, June 1981] The sound of a spray can being shaken
SHOOM [The Vision and The Scarlet Witch vol.2 #7, 1986] The sound of an energy beam hitting an object
SHOOOM [Fantastic Four #315] A zooming, rushing sound, as of a fireball
SHOOP [The Anomalies #1, 2000] The sound made by a floor opening beneath your feet
SHOOW [Man of War #8] The sound of an energy bolt

SHOOSH [Mantra vol.1 #7, 1994] The sound of flesh being torn off
SHPIKKLE [MAD #233, September 1982] The sound of soup
SHPLEP [MAD #212, January 1980] The sound of web fluid being shot from Spiderman's wrist
SHRABOOM [Star Hunters vol.2 #4, 1978] The sound of an explosion
SHRACK [2099 Unlimited vol.1 #2, 1993] The sound of an energy beam
SHRACKKKK [Venom: The Enemy Within vol.1 #1, 1994] A hitting sound
SHRACKKKKKK [Venom: The Enemy Within vol.1 #2, 1994] The sound of an explosion
SHRAK [Pitt #1, 1993] A hitting sound made with a mace: also SHRAKK [NFL SuperPro vol.1 #9, 1992] A hitting sound
SHRAKAKAKA KAKAKAKA [War Machine vol.1 #1, 1994] The sound of energy bolts
SHRAKK [Avengers West Coast Annual vol2 #8, 1993] The sound of energy bolts hitting their target
SHRAKOOM [The Anomalies #1, 2000] A sound of electronic weapon fire
SHRASHH [Batman #502, 1993] A crashing sound
SHRAZZAK [The Anomalies #1, 2000] A sound of electronic weapon fire
SHRIEK [New Kids On The Block: Step By Step, 1990] A cry of delight
SHRING [Star Hunters vol.2 #5, 1978] The peculiar sound of energy armor: [2099 Unlimited vol.1 #2, 1993] The sound of weapon fire hitting a wall
SHROOM also SHROOOOM [War Machine vol.1 #1, 1994] The sound of a missile in flight
SHROOOOM see SHROOM
SHROOOOOZH [Avengers West Coast Annual vol.2 #8, 1993] The sound of a device that, at once, repels stones and fuses them
SH-SHPRITZZZZ [MAD #209, September 1979] The spraying sound of an aerosol can
SHTOOOOOOOOOM [Avengers West Coast Annual vol.2 #8, 1993] The sound of an energy bolt
SHTUP [Clint #1, 1986] The sound of a bullet hitting upholstery
SHUK [The Solution vol.1 #2, 1993] The peculiar sound of a harpoon-like appendage piercing through a torso: [Knights of Pendragon #13] A punching, hitting sound
SHUMM [The Vision and The Scarlet Witch vol.2 #7, 1986] A hitting sound

SHUNK [The Adventures of Bayou Billy #2, 1989] The sound of an arrow hitting its target: [The Solution vol.1 #2, 1993] The sound of an arm being sliced off
SHVRAM [Star Hunters vol.2 #4, 1978] The sound of a space vehicle under attack being hit
SHWAK [Thunderstrike vol.1 #4, 1994] The sound of a body slammed against a wall
SHWAKK see SHWAK
SHWAM [2099 Unlimited vol.1 #3, 1993] A hitting sound
SHYEK [Dead Pool: The Circle Chase #4, 1993] The sound of a nullification field
SHYMMMMSS [Dead Pool: The Circle Chase #4, 1993] The sound of an inter-dimensional shift
SHZZTHSSSSSSSSSS [Dead Pool: The Circle Chase #4, 1993] The sound of a nullification field
SHZZZZT [ROM #34, 1982] The sound of electric fire
SIZZLE [The Adventures of Kool-Aid Man #6, 1989] A burning sound
SIZZLE SITZ [MAD #215, June 1980] The sound of a flare burning out
SKA-KOOM [War Machine vol.1 #1, 1994] The sound of an explosion
SKAKK [Dare Devil: The Man Without Fear vol.1 #2, 1993] The sound of a breaking guard rail
SKAPOW [Cable #5, 1993] A punching sound
SKA-RASHH [The Adventures of Bayou Billy #2, 1989] The sound of glass breaking
SKEEEE also SKREEEEE [Dare Devil #277] A screeching, skidding sound
SKLAZONCHO [MAD #227, December 1981] The sound made by sawing a body in half with a sword
SKLIK [MAD's Don Martin Cooks Up More Tales, 1976] The sound of a tear being formed
SKREEEEE see SKREEEE
SKLANG [Marvel Comics Presents vol.1 #11, 1993] The sound of breaking glass
SKLOOSH [MAD's Don Martin Cooks Up More Tales, 1976] The sound of a person rising up from a flood of tears
SKLOP [MAD #233, September 1982] The sound of soup
SKLORP [Ralph Snart Adventures #5, 1993] A belching sound
SKLORPSKX [Ralph Snart Adventures #5, 1993] A sound made by cutting into a rapidly decaying body
SKLUTCH [Steel #1.1994] The peculiar sound of a body parts being torn to pieces

SKOOM [War Machine vol.1 #1, 1994] The sound of an exploding artillery shell

SKOOMPH [War Machine vol.1 #1, 1994] The sound of an energy beam

SKRAAM [War Machine vol.1 #1, 1994] The sound of a body being slammed to the ground

SKRA-KABOOM [Darkhold #10, 1993] The sound of an explosion

SKRASH [ROM #37, 1982] The sound of breaking glass: [ROM #34, 1982] also SKRASHH [2099 Unlimited vol.1 #4, 1993] also SKRASSH also SKRAZH [Steel #1.1994] A crashing sound

SKRASHH see SKRASH

SKRASSH see SKRASH

SKRAWW also SKRAWWW also SKRAWWWKK [Avengers West Coast Annual vol.2 #8, 1993] The cry of a bird-man

SKRAWWW see SKRAWW

SKRAWWWKK see SKRAWW

SKRAZAK [War Machine vol.1 #1, 1994] The sound of electronic weapon fire

SKRAZH see SKRASH

SKREEE [Venom: Lethal Protector #3, 1993] also SKREEEEE [Superboy #154, 1969] A screeching sound, as of tires; [Mantra vol.1 #2, 1993] A rats cry of fear or pain: SKREEEE [G.I.Joe vol.1 #61, 1987] also SKREEEEEEEE [The Punisher: War Zone vol.1 #1, 1993] The screaming sound of tires spinning on asphalt

SKREEEE [Venom: Lethal Protector #3, 1993] The sound of a sonic grenade: [Star Wars Vol.1 #6 1977] the sound of a final agonized scream of flesh and metal

SKREEEE see SKREEE

SKREEEEE see SKREEE

SKREEEECH [The Adventures of Bayou Billy #3, 1990] A screeching sound, as of tires

SKREEEEEEE [MAD #218, October 1980] The sound of chalk on a chalkboard, similar to that of fingernails scraped on a chalkboard

SKREEEEEEEE [MAD #223, June 1981] An unspecified TV sound

SKREEEEEEEE see SKREEE

SKREEEK [MAD's Don Martin Cooks Up More Tales, 1976] The sound of a fast car pulling to a stop

skreek [Mantra vol.1 #2, 1993] A rats cry of fear or pain

SKREEK [MAD's Don Martin Cooks Up More Tales, 1976] The sound of trap door opening

SKREEKLE [MAD #217, September 1980] The sound of a badly made bird call
SKREEL [Ralph Snart Adventures #5, 1993] The sound of screeching tires
SKREEOW [Steel #1.1994] The sound of bullets passing close by
SKRIKSH [Knights of Pendragon #13] The sound of breaking glass
SKRISH [The Adventures of Bayou Billy #2, 1989] The sound of a cigar being butted out
SKROINCH [MAD #211, December 1979] The sound of a bus bench seat being torn off the floor: [MAD #212, January 1980] The sound of a body being run over
SKRONK [MAD #217, September 1980] The sound of a badly made bird call
SKRRKRREEEEEEEE [Avengers West Coast Annual vol.2 #8, 1993] The cry of a bird-man
SKRRR [Batman #502, 1993] The sound of cable being retracted
SKRUKK [Knights of Pendragon #13] A hitting sound
SKRUNCH [The Adventures of Bayou Billy #2, 1989] A crunching sound; [Avengers West Coast Annual vol.2 #8, 1993] The crunching sound of a rotating, drill shaped metal driver bearing into solid rock
SKUP [Batman #502, 1993] A kicking sound
SKWAKO [MAD #216, July 1980] The sound of a horse's kick
SKWAPPO [MAD #219, December 1980] The sound of a body hitting the ground after jumping off a high building
SKWEEK [MAD #178, October 1975] The sound of a cotton-tipped swab being used to clean an ear: [MAD #233, September 1982] The sound of a wooden leg being unscrewed
SLAM [Bobby Sherman #6, 1972] The sound of a door slam: [FREEX #7, 1994] The sound of a telephone receiver being hung up forcefully
SLAMDUNK [Star Wars Vol.1 #6 1977, ad] The imaginary sound of a basketball scoring forcefully
SLAMM [Avengers West Coast Annual vol.2 #8, 1993] A hitting sound
SLAP [Betty #40] The sound of an open handed blow
SLAPITY SLAP also **SLAPITY SLAP SLAP** [Clint: The Hamster Triumphant #1, 1986] The sound of multiple slaps
SLAPITY SLAP SLAP see SLAPITY SLAP
SLERP [Son of MAD, 1973] A drinking sound

SLLANK [Star Hunters vol.2 #4, 1978] The clanking sound of a metal door slamming shut
SLOK [The Night Man vol.1 #4, 1994] A hitting sound
SLOP [Bobby Sherman #6, 1972] The sound of paint being applied very quickly
SLORPH [Clint #1, 1986] The peculiar sound accompanying the emergence of an entity from beneath the earth
SLOTCH [MAD #233, September 1982] The sound of soup
slrrrk [Mantra vol.1 #7, 1994] A slurping sound
SLSSHH [Mantra: Infinity, 1995] The slicing sound of a bladed weapon
SLURP [The Adventures of Bayou Billy #2, 1989] A drinking sound, as with a straw: [MAD #249, September 1984] An eating sound
Slurp...crunch... [MAD #212, January 1980] Eating sounds
SLURRRP [Superboy #154, 1969] The slurping sound that a dog makes when licking someone's face off
SMACK [The Ren and Stimpy Show vol.1 #6, 1993] A punching sound: [Man of War #8] A kicking sound: [Mantra: Infinity, 1995] The sound of a slap: [The Adventures of Bayou Billy #4, 1990] also SMAK [Mantra vol.1 #7, 1994] A kissing sound: also SMAKK [Avengers West Coast Annual vol.2 #8, 1993] A hitting sound, as with a club
SMAK see SMACK
SMAKK see SMACK
SMASH [Man of War #8] A breaking sound: [Prototype vol.1 #6, 1994] The sound of breaking glass
SMEK [Ralph Snart Adventures #5, 1993] The sound of a punch in the mouth
S'MY [The Adventures of Captain Jack #7, 1987] Means "It's my"
SNAK [Dare Devil: The Man Without Fear vol. #4, 1994] The snapping sound of a broken neck
SNAKT [War Machine vol.1 #1, 1994] A mechanical sound made when fastening armor
SNAP [MAD #181, March 1976] The sound of twigs being broken: [Prototype vol.1 #6, 1994] The sound of a switch: [War Machine vol.1 #1, 1994] A mechanical sound, as made when fastening armor etc: [Dare Devil: The Man Without Fear vol.1 #3, 1993] The sound of neck vertebrae snapping: [Madballs vol.1 #7, 1987] The sound of an electric eel snapping its tail much like a whip; The sound of a finger snap: [The Adventures of Bayou Billy #3, 1990] The sound of restraining straps being broken: [Crackbusters #1, 1986] The sound of a pencil breaking: also SNAPP [The Adventures of

Bayou Billy #3, 1990] A snapping sound: [Dare Devil: The Man Without Fear vol.1 #4, 1994] A breaking sound, as of a blind man's cane
SNAPP see SNAP
Snf [Mantra vol.1 #5, 1993] A sniffing sound
SNIF [Clint #1, 1986] also SNIFF [The Ren and Stimpy Show vol.1 #6, 1993] A sniffing sound
SNIFF see SNIF
SNIK [G.I.Joe vol1 #104, 1990] The sound of a knife cutting a strap
SNIKK [Dare Devil: The Man Without Fear vol.1 #2, 1993] The sound of a switchblade opening
SNIKT [Incredible Hulk #180-181] The sound of Wolverine's Adamantium laced claws extruding from the backs of his hands
SNORT [New Kids On The Block: Step By Step, 1990] The sound of a bull snorting
SNUF [Ralph Snart Adventures #5, 1993] A snuffling sound
SOB [Madballs vol.1 #7, 1987] The sound of crying
SOCK [Fightin' Marines #145, 1979] also SOK [The Adventures of Bayou Billy #4, 1990] A punching sound
SOK [MAD #212, January 1980] A hitting sound
SOWCEWESS [Mantra vol.1 #5, 1993] Means "Sorceress"
SOWWY [Mantra vol.1 #5, 1993] Means "Sorry"
SPA-BASH [The Adventures of Bayou Billy #3, 1990] A splashing sound, as of a body dumped off a pier
SPAK [MAD's Don Martin Cooks Up More Tales, 1976] The sound of a body thrown from a height and hitting the ground: [G.I.Joe vol.1 #104, 1990] The sound of a bullet hitting wood: [2099 Unlimited vol.1 #2, 1993] The sound of gunfire hitting the ground
SPA-KRASHH [The Adventures of Bayou Billy #4, 1990] A crashing sound, as made when breaking through a skylight
SPAMAMP [MAD #233, September 1982] The sound of bodies in collision
SPANG [G.I.Joe vol.1 #61, 1987] The sound of a bullet hitting a metal object; The sound of a ricochet: [The Adventures of Bayou Billy #4, 1990] The sound of a bullet hitting the ground: [G.I.Joe vol.1 #104, 1990] The sound of tearing metal; The sound of sheet metal giving way: [The Adventures of Bayou Billy #4, 1990] The sound of a truck cab door being kicked open
SPASH [The Adventures of Bayou Billy #2, 1989] The sound of a gas canister

SPATZ also SPITZ [MAD #212, January 1980] The sputtering sound of no web fluid being shot from Spiderman's wrist
SPAZOOSH [MAD #219, December 1980] The sound of sudden flooding water
SPING [The Punisher: War Zone vol.1 #1, 1993] The sound of a bullet hitting armor
SPITZ see SPATZ
SPKANNG [Avengers West Coast Annual vol.2 #8, 1993] A hitting sound
SPLAATT also SPLAAATTTT [Fightin' Marines #145, 1979] A punching sound
SPLAK [MAD #211, December 1979] The sound of food being splashed: [The Night Man vol.1 #4, 1994] The sound of a stick breaking over someone's head
SPLANG [ROM #37, 1982] The sound of a punch on armor: [The Punisher: War Zone vol.1 #1, 1993] The sound of a 45 magnum hitting armor: [Avengers West Coast Annual vol.2 #8, 1993] The sound of a discus hitting an object
SPLASH [MAD #246, April 1984] The sound of splashing water: [ROM #37, 1982] also SPLASHH [Prototype vol.1 #6, 1994] The splashing sound of an body or object falling into water:
SPLASHH see SPLASH
SPLASHLE [MAD #232, July 1982] The sound of water being sprayed by a hose
SPLAT [Bobby Sherman #6, 1972] The sound an artist makes when slapping paint onto canvas: [MAD #188, January 1977] The sound of a bullet to the gut: [MAD #215, June 1980] The sound of an ax slicing through a head: [MAD #218, October 1980] The sound of a pie in the face: [MAD #224, January 1981] The sound of both barrels coming down on a head: [MAD #225, September 1981] The sound of a punch to the jaw: [Son of MAD, 1973] The sound a face makes when it is punched: [The Twisted Tantrum of the Purple Snit #1, 1980] The sound of an object splashing into water: [G.I.Joe vol.1 #104, 1990] The sound of a falling body hitting the street: [Dare Devil: The Man Without Fear vol.1 #2, 1993] The sound made when falling into wet snow: [The Ren and Stimpy Show vol.1 #6, 1993] The sound of a wet object hitting the ground
SPLATT [MAD Super Special 16, 1975] The sound of bodies colliding: [MAD #224, January 1981] also SPLATTT [Fightin' Marines #145, 1979] A punching sound
SPLATTT see SPLATT
SPLAZATCH [MAD #202, December 1978] The sound made by a sloppy paint brush

SPLAZITCH [MAD #202, December 1978] The sound made by a sloppy paint brush
SPLAZOOSH [MAD #217, September 1980] The sound of water being poured over a fire
SPLITCH also SPLOTCH [The Ren and Stimpy Show vol.1 #6, 1993] The peculiar sound of hairballs landing
SPLOIT [MAD #211, December 1979] The sound of food being thrown with a spoon
SPLOOSH [MAD's Don Martin Cooks Up More Tales, 1976] The sound of a large tear hitting the ground; The sound of a tear falling into a puddle of tears: [Mantra vol.1 #2, 1993] A splashing sound
SPLOP [MAD #233, September 1982] The sound of soup
SPLORCH [Darkhold: Pages f ROM the Book of Sins vol.1 #7, 1993] The sound of mnemonic ectoplasm as created by mutant hex power
SPLORK [MAD #211, December 1979] The sound of food being splashed
SPLORP [Mantra vol.1 #7, 1994] The sound of a rapidly decaying body
SPLOSH [Madballs vol.1 #7, 1987] A splashing sound
SPLOTCH see SPLITCH
SPLUBLE [MAD's Don Martin Cooks Up More Tales, 1976] The sound of a tear falling into a puddle of tears
SPLUT [Clint #1, 1986] The sound of splattering blood; [The Adventures of Bayou Billy #2, 1989] The sound made by spurting out a mouthful of water: [The Adventures of Bayou Billy #3, 1990] A spluttering sound, as when gasping for air: [Mantra vol.1 #2, 1993] A splattering sound: also SPLUTT [The Adventures of Bayou Billy #4, 1990] A splattering sound, as of a splashing paint can
SPLUTT see SPLUT
SPMAMP [MAD #229, March 1982] The sound of a sculptor working with a plastic material
SPOOF [MAD #217, September 1980] The sound of wood catching fire
SPOPPLE [MAD #212, January 1980] The sputtering sound of no web fluid being shot from Spiderman's wrist
SPRA-KOW [Darkhold: Pages from the Book of Sins vol.1 #7, 1993] The sound of a disruption of mnemonic ectoplasm by mutant hex power
SPRANG-WAH [The Adventures of Bayou Billy #2, 1989] The sound of a bullet ricocheting off metal
SPRAY [MAD #177, September 1975] The sound of an aerosol insecticide being sprayed

SPRIZZITZ [MAD #212, January 1980] The sound of a spray can

SPROING [MAD #217, September 1980] The sound of boards coming unsprung, as on a ship: [MAD #249, September 1984] The sound of a person jumping: [The Twisted Tantrum of the Purple Snit #1, 1980] The sound made when the spring of a spring loaded mechanism is released: also SPROOOING [The Ren and Stimpy Show vol.1 #6, 1993] A springing sound

SPROOOING see SPROING

SPRUK [Dare Devil: The Man Without Fear vol.1 #5, 1994] The sound of a bullet ripping through a forearm

SPTAK [Batman #502, 1993] The sound of electronic weapon fire hitting an object

SPUT-T SPUT-T CHUK-SPUT [Superboy #154, 1969] The sound of a sputtering outboard motor

SPWANG [MAD #216, July 1980] The sound of a bullet ricocheting

SPWAP [MAD #214, April 1980] The sound of a inked rubber stamp against a surface

SPWE also SPWEE [Mantra vol.1 #7, 1994] The sound of a bullet hitting the ground

SPWEE see SPWE

SPWEEE [Star Wars Vol.1 #6 1977] The sound of weapon fire

SQUIRT [Bobby Sherman #6, 1972] The sound of paint being squeezed from a tube

SQUISH [Bobby Sherman #6, 1972] The sound of paint being squeezed from a tube

SQULRRCH [Mantra vol.1 #7, 1994] A squelching sound

SRAAK [Thunderstrike vol.1 #4, 1994] The sound of breaking concrete

SRRAK [ROM #37, 1982] A hitting sound

SRREE [2099 Unlimited vol.1 #3, 1993] The sound of electronic weapon fire

SREEEEK [MAD #241, September 1983] The sound of rapid braking

SSHHFFOOOOOSH [Star Hunters vol.2 #5, 1978] The sound of an explosion

SSHUK [Darkhold: Pages from the Book of Sins vol.1 #7, 1993] The deployment sound of arrow-like missiles

SSQUEEEEEFROP [Dakota North vol.1 #3, 1986] The sound of air escaping from a balloon

SSSHHABA-BOOOOM [Star Hunters vol.2 #5, 1978] The sound of an explosion

SSSHHSSSS [ROM #43, 1983] A hissing sound

SSSHLORP [Darkhold #10, 1993] A slurping, oozing sound
SSSHOOOPPOOFF [Star Hunters vol.2 #4, 1978] The sound of the atmosphere rushing out of an escape port into the vacuum of space
SSSSHHHHHH [Star Hunters vol.2 #5, 1978] The sliding sound of an electric door
SSSSSS [Captain Marvel vol.1 #42, 1976] A sliding sound
SSSSSSSHHHH [Ragman: Cry of the Dead #1] The sound of running tap water
SSSSSSSSSSSS [Clint #1, 1986] A hissing sound
SSSSSSSSSSSSSHBLAMM [Captain Thunder and Blue Bolt #1] The sound of an explosion
SSSSSSSSSSWOSHH [Prototype vol.1 #6, 1994] The sound of an object rushing through air
SSSSSSSST [MAD #219, December 1980] The sound of water dousing flames
SSSSSSTTTT [The Adventures of Bayou Billy #2, 1989] The sound of a fuse, burning
SSSWWISSHHH [Attack #41, 1983] The sound of a bazooka rocket
SSZZHH [Star Hunters vol.2 #5, 1978] The sizzling sound of burning flesh
STOK [Batman #502, 1993] The sound of a bullet hitting its target
STOMPUH [Ralph Snart Adventures #5, 1993] A sound made by jumping on another person with both feet
STOOM [Thunderstrike vol.1 #2, 1994] The sound of a heavy footstep
STOONG [MAD #218, October 1980] The sound of a gargoyle landing on a salesman's head
SVASH [Venom: Lethal Protector #3, 1993] The sound of electronic weapon fire
SVBEEP [Cable #5, 1993] The sound of an electronic weapon
SWACK-K-K [The Adventures of Bayou Billy #2, 1989] A hitting sound
SWAP [MAD's Don Martin Cooks Up More Tales, 1976] The sound of a hand capturing an insect in flight
SWASHHH [Captain Atom #7] The sound of a bladed weapon slashing through air
SWAT [MAD's Don Martin Cooks Up More Tales, 1976] The sound made by pounding a fist into an open hand: [MAD #177, September 1975] The sound of a fly swatter in action
SWATHZZZWHOUMM [Dead Pool: The Circle Chase #4, 1993] The sound of an explosion
SWIF [NFL SuperPro vol.1 #9, 1992] A hitting sound

SWISH [MAD #246, April 1984] The sound of a sheet of paper being run through a machine: [Star Wars Vol.1 #6 1977, ad] The sound of a basketball passing through the hoop without touching the backboard or rim

SWOK [Thunderstrike vol.1 #4, 1994] The sound of a punch

SWOOOOP [The Ren and Stimpy Show vol.1 #6, 1993] A swooping sound

SWOOP [The Twisted Tantrum of the Purple Snit #1, 1980] A sound made by a thrown object in flight

SWOOSH [Ultraman vol.1 #2, 1994] The sound of an energy blast

SWUMP [Knights of Pendragon #13] A punching, hitting sound

SZHKK [Avengers West Coast Annual vol.2 #8, 1993] The sound of an energy beam

SZIT [Star Hunters vol.2 #4, 1978] The sound of electronic weapon fire

SZZIK [Star Hunters vol.2 #5, 1978] The peculiar sound of a thought activated handgun being drawn

SZZZZZT [Avengers West Coast Annual vol.2 #8, 1993] The peculiar sound of a communicard being destroyed

TA also **TAA** also **TAAA** also **TAAAAA** [The Adventures of Captain Jack #7, 1987] A trumpet sound

TAA see TA

TAAA see TA

TAAAAA see TA

TAA-DAAA [The Twisted Tantrum of the Purple Snit #1, 1980] A sound similar to that of a trumpet blast

TATARRA TARRA TARRA [Son of MAD, 1973] The sound of a bugle

TA TA TA TA [Our Fighting Forces #111, 1968] Bugle sounds

TAK [Dare Devil: The Man Without Fear vol.1 #5, 1994] The sound that a flipped coin makes when it bounces on a table: [War Machine vol.1 #1, 1994] A mechanical sound, as made when fastening armor

TAKA TAKA TAK [The Solution #5] The sound of typing, as on a computer keyboard

TANG [The Twisted Tantrum of the Purple Snit #1, 1980] A sound of people and equipment in operation, as might be heard on a construction site

TAP [Superboy #154, 1969] The sound of a light knock on a door: [Madballs vol.1 #7, 1987] A tapping sound: [Dare Devil #277] The sound of a blind man's cane tapping on a sidewalk

TAP TAP [Clint #1, 1986] The sound a pointer makes tapping on a wall map
TATTTA [Fightin' Marines #145, 1979] The sound of machine gun fire
TCHAKK [Avengers West Coast Annual vol.2 #8, 1993] A mechanical sound
TCHIKT [Dead Pool: The Circle Chase #4, 1993] The mechanical sound of a lock being picked
TCHOC [Lucky Luke: Canyon Apache, 1971] A punching sound
TCHUNK [Avengers West Coast Annual vol.2 #8, 1993] The sound of a thrown discus hitting someone in the head
TEE, HEE [The Adventures of Captain Jack #7, 1987] The sounds of laughter
THAK [MAD's Don Martin Cooks Up More Tales, 1976] The sound of a body thrown from a height and hitting the ground
THAKOMPH [War Machine vol.1 #1, 1994] The sound of weapon fire hitting a body
THAKT [Avengers West Coast Annual vol.2 #8, 1993] A sound made when tripping over a rock
THAMM [The Incredible Hulk vol.1 #229, 1978] A hitting sound
THAP [The Adventures of Bayou Billy #3, 1990] The sound of restraining straps being broken
THAPLOOF [MAD #216, July 1980] The sound of a horse landing after a jump
THCHTH [Dead Pool: The Circle Chase #4, 1993] The sound of a body hitting a wall
THHLORP [MAD #212, January 1980] The sound of Spiderman's web fluid being shot into a liquid
THHRRRP [Maxx #5, 1993] The sound made when blowing a raspberry
THHUD [Detective Comics vol.47 #529, 1983] A kicking sound
THITH-THITH-THITH [MAD #215, June 1980] The sound of helicopter blades
THKAM [War Machine vol.1 #1, 1994] The sound of an exploding artillery shell
THLIK [Star Hunters vol.2 #4, 1978] The sound of snapping fingers: [Star Hunters vol.2 #5, 1978] The sound of a switch
THLOOP [MAD #229, March 1982] The sound of a sculptor working with a plastic material
THLUCK [MAD #211, December 1979] The sound of one body being plucked from another

THMP [Mantra vol.1 #5, 1993] A thumping sound, as might be heard at a door
THOIP [MAD #227, December 1981] The sound of a sword blade being withdrawn from a body
THOK [2099 Unlimited vol.1 #4, 1993] A hitting sound
THOMP [G.I.Joe vol.1 #61, 1987] The sound of a foot striking someone: [G.I.Joe vol.1 #104, 1990] The sound a body makes when it bounces
THONGK [War Machine vol.1 #1, 1994] A punching sound
THONK [Clint #1, 1986] The sound of a ninja Star hitting an object
THOOM [Clint #1, 1986] The sound of a footfall; The sound of an explosion: [2099 Unlimited vol.1 #3, 1993] A hitting sound: [Thunderstrike vol.1 #2, 1994] The sound of an object being slammed to the ground
THOP [G.I.Joe vol.1 #104, 1990] The sound of an object hitting the palm of the hand: [The Adventures of Bayou Billy #3, 1990] The sound of restraining straps being broken
THPP [Dare Devil: The Man Without Fear vol.1 #4, 1994] The sound of an object fired from a slingshot being caught with a hand
THRAKAKAKAKAKA [War Machine vol.1 #1, 1994] The sound of energy bolts
THUBALUP THUBALUP THUBALUP [MAD #216, July 1980] The sound of a horse running
THRUMP [Knights of Pendragon #13] A thumping sound: [The Adventures of Bayou Billy #4, 1990] The sound of a falling body landing on the ground
THRUNCH [Batman #502, 1993] A crunching sound
THUD [Our Fighting Forces #111, 1968] The sound of a gunstock being used as a club: [Detective Comics vol.47 #529, 1983] A hitting sound: [Madballs vol.1 #7, 1987] The sound of an object hitting the ground: also THUDD [2099 Unlimited vol.1 #3, 1993] A hitting sound
THUDD see THUD
THUDOOM [2099 Unlimited vol.1 #4, 1993] The sound of a body forcefully hitting the ground
THUDUD [Crackbusters #1, 1986] The complex sound of two people being kicked at once
THUGAWUNK [MAD #219, December 1980] The sound of a body falling onto another body
THUK [Pitt #1, 1993] The sound that a mace makes when it hits a head: [Catwoman #6, 1994] A punching sound
THUMK [Mantra vol.1 #5, 1993] The sound of a heavy object hitting the ground

THUMP [G.I.Joe vol.1 #61, 1987] The sound of a kick to the head: [Dare Devil: The Man Without Fear vol.1 #2, 1993] A thumping sound, as of an object landing on the roof of a vehicle: [Mantra vol.1 #7, 1994] A hitting sound: [Crackbusters #1, 1986] The sound of a fist hitting a desk: [2099 Unlimited vol.1 #3, 1993] The sound of a heartbeat
THUMP THUMP [MAD #177, September 1975] The sound made by driving on a flat tire
THUNK [Our Fighting Forces #111, 1968] A kicking sound: [The Ren and Stimpy Show vol.1 #6, 1993] A hitting sound: [The Adventures of Bayou Billy #3, 1990] The sound made when a knife is planted into a tabletop
THUP [Captain Thunder and Blue Bolt vol.1 #1, 1987] The sound of helicopter rotors
THURCH [MAD #229, March 1982] The sound of a sculptor working with clay
THWAAASHHH [Thunderstrike vol.1 #4, 1994] The sound emanating from an energy beam
THWACK [MAD's Don Martin Cooks Up More Tales, 1976] The sound of flogging: [Superboy #154, 1969] The sound of a whip snapping: [G.I.Joe vol.1 #61, 1987] A hitting sound: also THWAK [Avengers West Coast Annual vol.2 #8, 1993] A punching sound
THWAK see THWACK
THWAMM [Avengers West Coast Annual vol.2 #8, 1993] A punching sound: [Thunderstrike vol.1 #4, 1994] A slamming sound
THWAT [MAD #244, January 1984] The sound of a paper clip shot with an elastic hitting a soft target
THWIP [MAD #211, December 1979] The sound of food being flung from a fork: [Spiderman #1] The sound of Spiderman's web line being shot: [G.I.Joe vol.1 #104, 1990] The sound of a bullet hitting wood
THWIT [MAD #246, April 1984] The sound of a poster being unfurled
THWOCK [MAD #219, December 1980] The sound of a body falling onto firefighter's trampoline
THWOK [MAD #244, January 1984] A stabbing sound
THWOKK [Cable #5, 1993] A punching sound
THWOOOM [Star Hunters vol.2 #4, 1978] The sound of an explosion
THWOP [MAD #212, January 1980] The sound of web fluid being shot from Spiderman's wrist
THWOW [Mantra vol.1 #5, 1993] Means "Throw"

THWRAKKAPWOMM [Cable #5, 1993] The sound of an explosion
THWUK [Darkhold: Pages from the Book of Sins vol.1 #7, 1993] The sound of a kick
TICK [Clint #1, 1986] The sound of a clock, as that attached to a time bomb
TIK [Darkhold #10, 1993] The click of a switch
TING [The Adventures of Bayou Billy #2, 1989] The sound of a bullet ricocheting off metal: [The Adventures of Bayou Billy #4, 1990] The sound of a bullet hitting the ground
TINKLE [Archie #407, 1993] A tinkling sound, as when a tail light is broken
TINKLE TINK INK [New Kids On The Block: Magic Summer Tour, 1990] The sound made by shaking a crystal chandelier
tinnng [Mantra vol.1 #7, 1994] A metallic ringing sound
TOC [Lucky Luke: Canyon Apache, 1971] A tapping sound
TOCK [Lucky Luke: Canyon Apache, 1971] A punching sound
TOK [The Punisher: War Zone vol.1 #1, 1993] The sound of a bullet hitting armor: [War Machine vol.1 #1, 1994] A knocking sound: [The Adventures of Bayou Billy #3, 1990] A hitting sound
TONG [MAD #244, January 1984] The sound of a brick landing on a head
TONK [Dare Devil #194] A sound made by hitting, as with a club
TOOB [MAD's Don Martin Cooks Up More Tales, 1976] The sound of a tuba
TOOM [Wonderman #12, 1992] A zooming sound: [2099 Unlimited vol.1 #3, 1993] A hitting sound
TOONG [MAD's Don Martin Cooks Up More Tales, 1976] A bouncing sound
TOOOOO [MAD #238, April 1983] The sound of an alarm
TRANG TRANG [Superboy #154, 1969] The sound of an alarm clock bell
TRIII also **TRIIIUUW** [The Adventures of Tintin: Explorers on the Moon, 1954] The sound sometimes heard while tuning a radio
TRIIIUUW see TRIII
TROMP [Ralph Snart Adventures #5, 1993] A sound made by jumping on another person with both feet
TTZZ [Dead Pool: The Circle Chase #4, 1993] A mechanical sound, as of parts coming undone
TUNGK [Dare Devil #194] A sound made by hitting, as with a club

TUNK [The Adventures of Bayou Billy #3, 1990] The hitting sound of an oak staff used as a weapon
TWANG [The Adventures of Bayou Billy #3, 1990] The sound of a bowstring
TWANNG [Madballs vol.1 #7, 1987] The sound of a catapult launching an object
TWEEN [MAD #216, July 1980] The sound of a bullet ricocheting
TWEEP [MAD's Don Martin Cooks Up More Tales, 1976] The sound of an object being shot out of a tuba
TWING [Attack #41, 1983] The sound of a bullet passing close by
TZAPT [Avengers West Coast Annual vol.2 #8, 1993] The sound made by a blast of energy
TZING [G.I.Joe vol.1 #104, 1990] The sound of a ricochet
TZNG [Mantra vol.1 #7, 1994] The sound of a bullet hitting the ground
TZZZZTT [ROM #34, 1982] The high frequency sound of an electric current
Editor's note: Comic words beginning with U are often cries of pain or indicative of sudden physical impact.
UFFT [Thunderstrike vol.1 #4, 1994] A cry of pain
Uggle...grunk...snik [MAD Super Special 16, 1975] Sounds made by a monster
UGH [MAD #202, December 1978] also Ugh [MAD #224, January 1981] A grunting sound indicating effort
Ugh see UGH
UGKH [The Punisher: War Zone vol.1 #1, 1993] A cry of pain
UHHNNNNN... [Detective Comics vol.47 #529, 1983] also UNNGHH also UNNHH also UNNNGHHH... also UUHH [Captain Marvel vol.1 #42, 1976] also UUUUUUUUUUUUUNNN... [Star Hunters vol.2 #4, 1978] A groaning sound
UHMMMMM [The Adventures of Bayou Billy #2, 1989] A kissing sound
UHNNFF [Dare Devil: The Man Without Fear vol.1 #3, 1993] also UNNGHH [Fantastic Four #315, 1988] A grunting sound
ULP [Cold Blooded Chamelion Commando #1, 1986] A gulping or swallowing sound
UM,HMMM [The Adventures of Captain Jack #7, 1987] A sound made to indicate agreement or "Yes"
UMMPH [MAD Super Special Number 31, Summer 1980] The sound of a baseball hitting a face

UNGGG [Mantra vol.1 #7, 1994] A grunting sound, as when hit

UNGH [2099 Unlimited vol.1 #4, 1993] also UNNGH [Mantra vol.1 #2, 1993] An exclamation caused by receiving a sudden impact to the body

UNH [The Adventures of Captain Jack #7, 1987] A grunting sound indicating "Yes", "What" etc

UNKLIK [MAD #232, July 1982] The sound of a lock being opened

UNNGH see UNGH

UNNGHH see UHNNFF

UNNGHH see UHHNNNNN...

UNNH [The Adventures of Bob Hope #95, 1965] The sound of a woman swooning from a yummy super hero kiss: also UNNHH also UNNNGHH [Avengers West Coast Annual vol.2 #8, 1993] also UNNNH [The Punisher: War Zone vol.1 #1, 1993] A cry of pain

UNNHH see UHHNNNNN...

UNNNGHH see UNNH

UNNNGHHH... see UHHNNNNN...

UNNNH see UNNH

UNPH [Batman #502, 1993] A sound made by a person being hit

URF [Superboy #154, 1969] The sound of a dog's bark

URK [Cold Blooded Chamelion Commando #1, 1986] A sound made by a person when hit hard

URP [MAD #230, April 1982] A video game sound

URPH [The Adventures of Bayou Billy #2, 1989] The sound a person makes when they are hit in the stomach

URP-TSTFOOF [MAD's Don Martin Cooks Up More Tales, 1976] The sound of very noxious belch

URRGG [Avengers West Coast Annual vol.2 #8, 1993] A gurgling sound

URRUGH [Thunderstrike vol.1 #4, 1994] A cry of pain

UUHH see UHHNNNNN...

UUNNNH... [Darkhold #10, 1993] A moaning sound

UUURRGGGHH [Clint #1, 1986] A cry

UUUUURP [Prototype vol.1 #1, 1994] A cry of pain

UUUUUUUUUUUUUNNN... see UHHNNNNN..

VAA-ROOOMM [The Adventures of Bayou Billy # 2, 1989] also VARHOOOOMM [The Adventures of Bayou Billy # 4, 1989] The sound of a monster truck engine: also VAROOMMM [MAD #225, September 1981] The sound of a car accelerating: also VAROOM ROWM [MAD #209, September 1979] The sound of high speed traffic

VARHOOOOMM see VAA-ROOOMM
VAROOMMM see VAA-ROOOMM
VAROOM ROWM see VAA-ROOOMM
VA-THROOOOM [G.I.Joe vol.1 # 60, 1987] The sound of a launching missile
VING [The Adventures of Bayou Billy # 2, 1989] The sound of a bullet ricocheting off metal
VIP [Attack # 41, 1983] The sound of a bullet passing close by
VLURSH [Mantra vol.1 # 7, 1994] The sound made by rapidly decaying flesh
VOOM [MAD #218, October 1980] The sound of an explosion
VOOMAROOMA [MAD #222, April 1981] The sound of a fast vehicle
VOOOOSH see VOOSH
VOOOSH see VOOSH
VOOSH also VOOOSH [Madballs vol.1 # 7, 1987] The sound of an object rushing through air: also VOOOOSH [Wonderman # 12, 1992] The sound of a rocket in flight
VOOT [Pitt # 1, 1993] The sound of an alarm
VOWM [MAD's Don Martin Cooks Up More Tales, 1976] The sound of a person hurtling through the air to the ground
VRAM also VRM [New Kids On The Block: Magic Summer Tour, 1990] A helicopter sound
VREE also VREEEEEEEEEEEE also VREEEEEEEEEEEEEEET [ROM # 34, 1982] also VREEEET [ROM # 35, 1982] also VREET [ROM # 37, 1982] also VREEEEEE [ROM # 43, 1983] The sound made by a Crimson Energy Beam
VREEEEEE see VREE
VREEEEEEEEEEEE see VREE
VREEEEEEEEEEEEEEEET see VREE
VREEEET see VREE
VREET see VREE
VRM see VRAM
VROOM [MAD #222, April 1981] The sound of a vacuum cleaner: also VROOOM [Superboy # 154, 1969] The sound made by a sudden force applied to an object [Madballs vol.1 # 7, 1987]: [Dare Devil: The Man Without Fear vol.1 # 2, 1993] The sound of a motor: also VROOOOMM [The Adventures of Bayou Billy # 3, 1990] The sound of a revving motor: also V-ROOOM [MAD #211, December 1979] The sound of a speeding car
VROOM SPOOSH [MAD Super Special Number 31, Summer 1980] The sound of water coming out of a shower head

V-ROOOM see VROOM
VROOOM see VROOM
VROOOOMM see VROOM
VROOSH [ROM # 43, 1983] The sound made by rocket pods: also VROOSHH [The Adventures of Bayou Billy # 2, 1989] The sound of a flame thrower: also VROOOSH [Avengers West Coast Annual vol.2 # 8, 1993] A rushing sound; The sound of a space ship moving through an atmosphere
VROOSHH see VROOSH
VROOOSH see VROOSH
VRUUM [Avengers West Coast Annual vol.2 # 8, 1993] The sound made by an airborne vehicle
VRZM also VRZMM also VRZMMM also VRZMMMMMM also VRZMMVRZMM [NFL SuperPro vol.1 # 9, 1992] The sound of some thing suddenly coming into existence in this dimension
VRZMM see VRZM
VRZMMM see VRZM
VRZMMMMMM see VRZM
VRZMMVRZMM see VRZM
VSSHHHH [2099 Unlimited vol.1 # 4, 1993] The sound of an object moving rapidly through air
VVVVVSSSSSS [Star Hunters vol.2 # 5, 1978] The buzzing sound of a flying vehicle
VWAM [Ultraman vol.1 # 2, 1994] A sound of weapon fire
VWAP [Ultraman vol.1 # 2, 1994] A sound of weapon fire
VWAP GAA-RIEP VROOM [Ultraman vol.1 # 2, 1994] The peculiar sounds of a robot body being destroyed
VZZZT also VZZZZT also VZZZZZZZZZZZT [Cable # 5, 1993] The buzzing sound of a parabolic slicing blade in flight
VZZZZT see VZZZT
VZZZZZZZZZZZT see VZZZT
WAA [MAD #212, January 1980] The sound of crying
WAK [The Ren and Stimpy Show vol.1 #6, 1993] A slapping or hitting sound
WAP [MAD #212, January 1980] The sound made by landing on one's rear while roller skating
WEEEEEE [MAD #238, April 1983] The sound of a siren
WEEEEEEEEEEEE [MAD #211, December 1979] The sound of an alarm
WEEEOOOOWEEEOOOWEEEOOOO also WEEOOOOWEEEOOOOWEEE [MAD #215, June 1980] also WEEOOOWEEE [MAD #222, April 1981] also WEEOOOWEEEOOOOWEEEOOOO [MAD #219, December 1980] A siren

WEEOOOOWEEEOOOOWEEE see WEEEOOOOWEEEOOOWEEEOOOO
WEEOOOWEEE see WEEEOOOOWEEEOOOWEEEOOOO
WEEOOOWEEEOOOOWEEEOOOO see WEEEOOOOWEEEOOOWEEEOOOO
WHACK [Madballs vol.1 #7, 1987] A hitting sound made by banging on a door
WHAM [Our Fighting Forces #111, 1968] The sound of a collision; The sound of an explosion: [Madballs vol.1 #7, 1987] The sound of an object hitting the ground: [Rag #1] A hitting sound: [Darkhold #10, 1993] The sound made by a slamming fist: [Pitt #1, 1993] The slamming sound of a body against a wall: [Madballs vol.1 #7, 1987] A banging sound, as upon a door: also WHAMB [Venom: Lethal Protector #3, 1993] The sound of an explosion: also WHAMM [G.I.Joe vol.1 #6, 1987] The sound of a heavy gun being fired
WHAMB see WHAM
WHAMM see WHAM
WAMP [MAD #221, March 1981] A sound made during lovemaking
WHANG [War Machine vol.1 #1, 1994] A sound made by punching composite polyalloy
WHAP [G.I.Joe vol.1 #61, 1987] also WHAPP [Detective Comics vol.47 #529, 1983] also WHAPPP [G.I.Joe vol.1 #60, 1987] A hitting sound; A kicking sound
WHAPP see WHAP
WHAPPP see WHAP
WHAZRASH [Star Hunters vol.2 #4, 1978] The sound of weapon fire vaporizing its target
WHEEEE [Attack #41, 1983] The sound of a mortar shell in flight
WHEEEEEEE [Betty #40, 1996] Imitative of a child's cry of delight with speed
WHIP [Ralph Snart Adventures #5, 1993] The sound of an object being thrown
WHIR [MAD #212, January 1980] The sound of an electric motor on a swing stage
WHIRRR [Star Hunters vol.2 #4, 1978] The whirring sound of an electronic instrument
WHIRRRR also WHIRRRRRRRR [The Anomalies #1, 2000] A mechanical sound made by a moving platform
WHIRRRRRRRR see WHIRRRR
WHIR WHIR [MAD #178, October 1975] The sound of a push lawn mower

WHIZZ [Betty #40] also **WHIZZZ** [Detective Comics vol.47 #529, 1983] The sound of an object moving quickly
WHOMP [Attack #41, 1983] The sound of an explosion: [G.I.Joe vol.1 #60, 1987] A hitting sound
WHOOM [Madballs vol.1 #7, 1987] The sound of an explosion
WHOOOMMMM [Venom: The Enemy Within vol.1 #1, 1994] A hitting sound
WHOOOOOOOOOOOOOOOOOOOOOOO [MAD #223, June 1981] An unspecified TV sound
WHOOPEE [MAD #214, April 1980] A cheer
WHOOPWHOOP [MAD #223, June 1981] also WHOOPWHOOPWHOOPWHOOPWHO [MAD #223, June 1981] A siren sound
WHOOPWHOOPWHOOPWHOOPWHO see WHOOPWHOOP
WHOOSH [Darkhold #10, 1993] The sound of an object moving swiftly: [MAD #209, September 1979] The sound of a fire starting: [MAD #224, January 1981] The sound of a gust of wind
WHREEP see WHREEEP
WHREEEP [Star Hunters vol.2 #4, 1978] also WHREEP [Star Hunters vol.2 #5, 1978] The sound of electronic weapon fire
WHRRRR [Prototype vol.1, 1994] A whirring sound
WHRRRRR-TCHAK [War Machine vol.1 #1, 1994] The spinning sound of a cylinder in a handgun
WHUD [Dare Devil: The Man Without Fear vol.1 #2, 1993] A punching sound
WHUDWHUD [Dare Devil: The Man Without Fear vol.1 #2, 1993] The sound of multiple punches, a combo
WHUK [Captain Thunder and Blue Bolt #1] The sound of falling rock: [Dare Devil: The Man Without Fear vol.1 #4, 1994] A kicking sound: [Knights of Pendragon #13] also WHUKK [Knights of Pendragon #13] A punching sound
WHUKK see WHUK
WHUMF [Betty #40, 1996] The sound made by landing on the ground on one's rear end
WHUMP [Our Fighting Forces #111, 1968] The sound of colliding bodies: [Detective Comics vol.47 #529, 1983] A kicking sound; A slamming sound, as of a door: [MAD #225, September 1981] The sound of a punch to the jaw
WHUNK [MAD #244, January 1984] A hitting sound
WHUTCH [Knights of Pendragon #13] The sound of an ax swung through the air

WOK [Avengers West Coast Annual vol.2 #8, 1993] A punching sound
WOM [Avengers West Coast Annual vol.2 #8, 1993] A punching sound: [The Punisher: War Zone vol.1 #1, 1993] The sound of a car landing on its side
WOMO [The Night Man vol.1 #4, 1994] A hitting sound
WOMP [Madballs vol.1 #7, 1987] The sound of banging on a door
WOO WO WOWOW also WOOW OW OW OW [The Adventures of Tintin: Explorers on the Moon, 1954] The sound of a dog barking
WOO-WOO-WOOO [Star Hunters vol.2 #5, 1978] The sound of a siren
WOOOSH [ROM #34, 1982] The rushing sound of a rapid movement
WOOUUIIIIII [The Adventures of Tintin: Explorers on the Moon, 1954] The sound that a radio makes while being tuned
WOOW OW OW OW see WOO WO WOWOW
WOOWOOWOOWOO [Ralph Snart Adventures #5, 1993] A whooping cry of excitement
WRAKT [Detective Comics vol.47 #529] The sound of a kick to a wooden crate
WREEEP [Star Hunters vol.2 #5, 1978] The sound of electronic weapon fire
WROK [Venom: Lethal Protector #3, 1993] A punching sound
WRRZZ [MAD #188, January 1977] The sound of a band saw
WUD [Ralph Snart Adventures #5, 1993] A punching sound, as to the stomach
WUMF [Ralph Snart Adventures #5, 1993] The sound of a body hitting a wall
WUMP [Captain Marvel vol.1 #42, 1976] also WUMPP [Dare Devil: The Man Without Fear vol.1 #2, 1993] The sound of a falling body landing on the ground: [MAD #238, April 1983] The sound of a kick to the groin
WUMPP see WUMP
WUNK [MAD #175, June 1975] The sound of a kick
YAA [Star Wars Vol.1 #6 1977] The sound of a desperate shout: [Dare Devil: The Man Without Fear vol.1 #4, 1994] also [Dare Devil: The Man Without Fear vol.1 #5, 1994] also YAAAAAAGH [FREEX #7, 1994] also YAAG [Dare Devil: The Man Without Fear vol.1 #3, 1993] also YAGGGGHHHHHHHH [Venom: The Enemy Within vol.1 #1, 1994] A cry of pain

YA-A-A [Secret Origins DC vol.2 #7] also YAAAAA [Avengers West Coast Annual vol.2 #8, 1993] The diminishing cry of a falling person, as heard from some other point
YAAAAA see YA-A-A
YAAAAAAAAHHH also YAYAYAHHH also YAYAYAYAYAHHH [Lucky Luke: Canyon Apache, 1971] An Indian war cry
YAAAAAAGH see YAA
YAAAGH [MAD #227, December 1981] A cry of pain
YAAAHH [MAD #177, September 1975] The sound of people screaming on a carnival ride: [MAD #227, December 1981] A cry of terror or fear
YAAAIIIEEEE [MAD #217, September 1980] A diminishing cry of a person falling a great distance
YAAG see YAA
YAAH [MAD Super Special 16, 1975] A cry of frustration
YAF-SLISH [MAD's Don Martin Cooks Up More Tales, 1976] The struggling sound of a dying man
YAGGGGHHHHHHHH see YAA
YAH-HOOOOOOO see YAHOO
YAHOO [Captain Marvel vol.1 #42, 1976] also YAH-HOOOOOOO [Betty #40, 1996] A cry or shout of satisfaction, delight, pleasure, joie de vivre etc as sometimes expressed by cowboys and other people of action
YAK [MAD #211, December 1979] A fighting cry
YAYAYAHHH see YAAAAAAAAHHH
YAYAYAYAYAHHH see YAAAAAAAAHHH
Yecccch [MAD #224, January 1981] also YECCCH [MAD #225, September 1981] also YECCH [MAD #227, December 1981] A sound indicating distaste, as in "Yuck!"
YECCCH see Yecccch
YECCH see Yecccch
YEE-OUCH [The Solution #5] A cry of pain
YEEOOW see YEOW
YEEOWWW see YEOW
YEH [Fightin' Marines #145, 1979] Means "Yes"
YEOW also YOW [The Adventures of Tintin: Explorers on the Moon, 1954] also YEEOOW [Madballs vol.1 #7, 1987] also YEEOWWW [MAD #222, April 1981] A cry of pain, fear, protest etc
YEOWWWWW [MAD #217, September 1980] The sound a person makes when falling on their head
YIII [The Adventures of Bob Hope #95, 1965] also YIIII [MAD #224, January 1981] An expression of shock or surprise
YIIII see YIII

YIIKES [MAD #230, April 1982] An exclamation indicating a blunder
YIPPY [MAD #214, April 1980] A cheer
YOO HOO [G.I.Joe vol.1 #60, 1987] A cry used to attract attention
YOW see YEOW
YUG [MAD #221, March 1981] A sound made during lovemaking
YUM [MAD #249, September 1984] An eating sound
YYYAAHHAAAGGHH [Venom: Lethal Protector #3, 1993] A cry of pain
YYYY [Avengers West Coast Annual vol.2 #8, 1993] A cry of pain

Editor's note: Comic words beginning with Z are often related to high frequency energy manifestations.

Z see ZZZZ...
ZACHITTY [MAD #229, March 1982] A sweeping sound
ZANNNNNG [MAD #227, December 1981] The sound of a radial arm saw blade
ZAP [MAD #227, December 1981] The sound of a bolt of lightning
Zap...pow [MAD's Don Martin Cooks Up More Tales, 1976] Sounds punctuating a dance move
ZAPPP [MAD #209, September 1979] The sound of an energy bolt
ZAPPPPPPP [MAD #209, September 1979] The sound of an energy bolt
ZAPT [Avengers West Coast Annual vol.2 #8, 1993] The sound made by an electrically charged arrow hitting armor
ZAPOW [The Anomalies #1, 2000] A sound of electronic weapon fire
ZAZZIK [MAD #231, June 1982] The sound made by dialing a rotary telephone
ZEEZEE [The Ren and Stimpy Show #6, 1993] A tuning sound, as of a radio transmitter
ZERK [Dare Devil: The Man Without Fear vol.1 #2, 1993] A snoring sound
ZARCH [Pitt #1, 1993] The sound of gunfire
ZICH [MAD #229, March 1982] A sweeping sound
ZIK [MAD #231, June 1982] also ZIKKA [MAD #231, June 1982] also ZIZZAK [MAD #231, June 1982] The sound made by dialing a rotary telephone
ZIK ZIK ZIK [MAD #181, March 1976] The sound of flint being used to create sparks
ZIKKA see ZIK

ZING [Attack #41, 1983] The sound of a passing bullet
ZIP [MAD #177, September 1975] The sound of a flight suit being zipped up
ZIT ZITZIZIZIZZZZZ [MAD #212, January 1980] The sound of an object that should be sticking, slipping down a wall instead
ZIZZAK see ZIK
ZRAKT [Pitt #1, 1993] The sound of gunfire
ZLIKT [Cable #5, 1993] The sound of a parabolic slicing blade cutting through flesh
ZOAM [Captain Marvel vol.1 #42, 1976] The sound of an energy bolt
ZONK [MAD #188, January 1977] The sound of a karate chop
ZOOM [Betty #40, 1996] The sound of an object traveling very quickly: also ZOOOOOMM [MAD #241, September 1983] The sound of a car speeding away
ZOOOOOMM see ZOOM
ZOOOSHHH [Captain Atom #7] The sound of an object moving or expanding at great speed
ZOWIE [Betty #40, 1996] An energetic exclamation of pleasure etc
ZPFT also ZVIPT [Venom: The Enemy Within vol.1 #1, 1994] The sound accompanying a sudden disappearance in a blast of pure cosmic energy
ZRAAK [Darkhold #10, 1993] The sound of an interruption in a laser beam
ZRAK [Avengers West Coast Annual vol.2 #8, 1993] The sound of an energy bolt
ZRASH [Star Hunters vol.2 #5, 1978] The sound of electronic weapon fire hitting the floor
ZURK [Dare Devil: The Man Without Fear vol.1 #3, 1993] A snoring sound
ZVIPT see ZPFT
ZVVPPTTTT [Venom: The Enemy Within vol.1 #1, 1994] The sound accompanying a sudden reappearance in a blast of pure cosmic energy
ZWAZASH [Star Hunters vol.2 #4, 1978] The sound of gunfire
ZWIP [The Solution vol.1 #2, 1993] The sound of a bazooka or rocket launcher
ZWIT [MAD #222, April 1981] The sound of a combination lock being turned
ZWOOSH [The Ren and Stimpy Show #6, 1993] The zooming, rushing sound of someone moving very quickly

ZZ also ZZZ also ZZZZ also ZZZZZ also ZZZZZZ also ZZZZZZZZ [MAD's Don Martin Cooks Up More Tales, 1976] The sound of a beetle in flight: ZZZT [MAD's Don Martin Cooks Up More Tales, 1976] The sound of a beetle ending it's flight by flying into an open mouth: also [MAD #223, June 1981] The sound of light snoring
ZZAM [Man of War #8] The sound of an energy bolt
ZZAT [The Solution vol.1 #2, 1993] The sound of gunfire
ZZCHATHZZ [Cable #5, 1993] The sound of an energy discharge
ZZHIP [FREEX #7, 1994] The zipping sound of bullets passing close by
ZZRAAK [Darkhold #10, 1993] The electrical sound accompanying an electrocution
ZZRAK also ZZRAKK also ZZRARKT also ZZRRAKKK also ZZWAKKT also ZZWAKK [Captain Thunder and Blue Bolt #1] The sound of an electric bolt
ZZRAKK see ZZRAK
ZZRAKSH [Star Hunters vol.2 #4, 1978] The sound of electronic weapon fire
ZZRAP [The Anomalies #1, 2000] A sound of electronic weapon fire
ZZRARKT [Captain Thunder and Blue Bolt #1, 1987] The sound of a bolt of energy
ZZRASH [Star Hunters vol.2 #5, 1978] A sound of weapon fire hitting its target
ZZRRAKKK [Captain Thunder and Blue Bolt #1, 1987] The sound of a bolt of energy
ZZT also ZZTZZT [Dead Pool: The Circle Chase #4, 1993] A mechanical sound, as of parts coming undone
ZZTZZT see ZZT
ZZVT [Cable #5, 1993] The sound of a parabolic slicing blade in flight
ZZWAKKT [Captain Thunder and Blue Bolt #1, 1987] The sound of a bolt of energy
ZZZ see ZZ
ZZZCHATHZZZ [Cable #5, 1993] The sound of an energy discharge
ZZZINK [Detective Comics vol.47 #529, 1983] A sound made by an arrow hitting a wall
ZZZOTZH [Star Hunters vol.2 #5, 1978] The sound of electronic weapon fire
ZZZRAKK [Avengers West Coast Annual vol.2 #8, 1993] The sound of an electrical discharge
ZZZRATCH [Star Hunters vol.2 #5, 1978] The sound of electronic weapon fire hitting its target

ZZZT see ZZ

ZZZT [Star Hunters vol.2 #5, 1978] The sound of electronic weapon fire: [Dead Pool: The Circle Chase #4, 1993] A mechanical sound, as of parts coming undone

ZZZWAKK [Captain Thunder and Blue Bolt #1] The sound of an electric bolt

ZZZZ... [The Adventures of Tintin: Explorers on the Moon, 1954] also ZZZZZZ [Lucky Luke: Canyon Apache, 1971] also Z [Ralph Snart Adventures #5, 1993] A sound made by a sleeping person

ZZZINK [Detective Comics vol.47 #529, 1983] The sound made by an arrow hitting a wall

ZZZZ see ZZ

ZZZZ [MAD #229, March 1982] The sound of a buzzer

ZZZZT [MAD #202, December 1978] A sound made when electrical wires are torn away

ZZZZTHSHYEEK [Dead Pool: The Circle Chase #4, 1993] The sound of the nullification of a weapon of war by use of a nullification field; see SHYEK

ZZZZZ see ZZ

ZZZZZT [Avengers West Coast Annual vol.2 #8, 1993] The sound of an energy beam

ZZZZZZ see ZZZZ.

ZZZZZZIZZZZ [MAD #244, January 1984] The sound of a roller skate as it rolls away after having tripped over it

ZZZZZZZ see ZZ

ZZZZZZZTZZZTZZZ [Dead Pool: The Circle Chase #4, 1993] A mechanical sound, as of parts coming undone

ZZZZZZZZ see ZZ

ZZZZ ZZZZZ also ZZZZZ ZZZ [MAD #241, September 1983] The sound of a bee buzzing

ZZZZZZ ZZZ see ZZZZ ZZZZZ

BZZURKK!

The Thesaurus of Champions

Complete with Suggested Spellings & Inspired Variations Thereby Assembling the Most Comprehensive List of Onomatopoeic Synonyms Available at Any Time Past or Present & Including Phoneticisms Never Before Published in Any Lexicon

Compiled by Kevin J. Taylor

Air Vehicle
  Airplane: HUMMMMM, KIKKI-TIKKI-KIKKI-TIKKI, KIPUCKATA SPOP [see Flight, Speed]
  Helicopter: CHAKK-CHAKK-CHAK-CHAK, CHAK-A-CHAK-AKK-CHK CHK-CHK, DUBDUBDUBDUBDUBDUB, THITH-THITH-THITH, THUP, VRAM, VRM [see Flight, Speed]
Alarm: AAH-OOOH-GAH, AGOOOOOGAH, AOOG, AOOGAOOGAOOO, AROGAH, AROOGA, AROOGAH, AROOGAHAROOGAH, BEEP, BEEEEP, BEEEEEP, BEEEEEEEP, BING, BONG, BREEP, BUZZ, BZZZZZZZZZZZZZZZZZCRACK, CLANG, DOOOT, DRRRRIINNNNGGG, EEEEEE, EEEEEEEEEE, INGALINGALINGALINGALING, PING, RING, RRIIINNNNGGG, RRRRIINNNNGGG, TOOOOO, TRANG TRANG, VOOT, WEEEEEEEEEEEE, WEEEEEEEEEEEEEZZZZ [see Bell, Buzzing, Horn, Indicator, Signal, Siren, Radar]
Animal
  Bird: BEEP, CAWEE, GLAWK, GLEEP, GOBBLE GOBBLE, HONK, HOOT, KAW, KAWW, QUACK WAAK WAAK, SKRAWW, SKRAWWW, SKRAWWWKK, SKREEEEEE, SKREEKLE, SKRONK, SKRRKRREEEEEEEE, SKRAWW, SKRAWWW, SKRAWWWKKm TWEET TWEET, T-WIT, TWITTER
  Bull: MMMOOOOO, SNORT
  Cat: HISSS, HISSSSSS, MEOROWWWGHHH, Meorowwwgssh, MEOW, MROW, PPRRRR, PRAYKKK
  Chamelion: BLAP
  Dog: ARF, ARFF, A-RUFF, AROOOO, ARRRRROOOOO, BOW WOW, GRRR, GRR, GRRR, GRRR..., GRRRR, GRRRRRR..., GRRRRR, H-H-H, OOWW, OWOOO, R-RRR, R-R-R-R, R-R-R-R-R, ROWF, ROWFF, ROWRR, RR-UFF, RROWF, RUFF, SLURRRP, URF, WOO WO WOWOW, WOOW OW OW OW
  Electric eel: SNAP
  Frog: RIBBIT
  Horse: SKWAKO, THAPLOOF, THUBALUP THUBALUP THUBALUP
  Insect: BZZZ, BZZZZZ, ZZ, ZZZ, , ZZZT, ZZZZ, ZZZZZ, ZZZZZZZ, ZZZZ ZZZZZ, ZZZZZZ ZZZ
  Rat: SKREEEEE, skreek
  Sea serpent: RRRRAARGH
Applause: CLAP, CLAP CLAP

Armor: CHIK, CLAK, CLIK, KLIK, SHRING, SNAKT, SNAP, TAK [see Mechanical, Metal]
Axe: CHIP, CHOP, KATRANG, PIK PIK PIK, SPLAT, WHUTCH [see Blade, Chainsaw, Clubbing, Cutting, Martial Arts, War Cry, Weapon]
Balloon: FFFRRRAAPFT, FWHEEEEE, POP, SSQUEEEEEFROP [see Bouncing, Bubble, Popping, Spring]
Belching / Burping: BELLLCCH, BRAX, BURP, BURPXK, SKLORP, URP-TSTFOOF [see Body, Coughing, Farting, Laxative, Sneezing, Vomit]
Bell: BING, BONG, BING BONG, BONNG, DANG, DINGALINGA, DINGILINGA, D-DING, DANG, DING, DING DONG, DINGG, DING GING, DONG, DRRRRIIINNNNGGG, GADONG, GALOON, GLANGADANG, GLONG, GONG, TRANG TRANG [see Alarm, Buzzing, Horn, Indicator, Signal, Siren, Radar, Telephone]
Bird see Animal
Blade: CHAK, GUK, SNIKK, SWASHHH, THUP, VZZZT, VZZZZT, VZZZZZZZZZZT, ZLIKT, ZZVT [see, Chainsaw, Cutting, Dieing, Saw, Slashing, Weapon]
Blast: BOOM, CHAT-CHOOM, FASH, FZZT, FZZZZZ, FZZZZZZZZ, HAUGGHHHHH, HAUGGHHHHHMM, HAUUGGGGHHHHHHHH, HAUUGGGHHHHHHH, KZAKK, RAUGHHHHHH, TZAPT, ZPFT, ZVIPT, ZVVPPTTTT [see Bullet, Energy, Explosion, Gun, Missile, Mortar, Thunder, Volcano, Weapon]
Body: BLINK-DIT, BLINK, CRICK CRACK, ERGHHH, GAACCK, gagg, GAGG, Gaggh...., GAGGAK-THOOF, GAK, GLAKK, GORE, HHUURGG, HIC, KLIK, KRRIK, KTHUMP, PUFF, SCRATCH SCRATCH, SNAK, SNAP, Snf, SNIF, SNUF, SPLUT, THLIK, THUMP [see Belching, Coughing, Farting, Laxative, Sneezing, Vomit]
Bouncing: BOINK, KIT-TOONG, KITTOONG, PEK, PEK PEK PEK, POIK, POINK, TAK, THOMP, TOONG [see Balloon, Bubble, Popping, Spring]
Brake: EEEECCCHH, SKEEEE, SKREEEEE, SKREEE, SKREEEEE, SKREEEE, SKREEEEEEEE, SKREEEK, SREEEEK [see Vehicle]
Breaking: CRACK, CRAACK, CRAAKK, CRAASH, CRACK, CRASH, CRASHH, FOOF, KASHH, KATL, KHRASSH, KRACK, KRAACK, KRA-ACK, KRAAK, KRAK, KRAKC, KRAKK, KRASH, KRASHH, KRESHH, KRRKK, PLINK, POP, SKAKK, SKRASH, SKRIKSH, SMASH, SNAP, SNAPP, SPLAK, SRAAK, THAP, THOP [see Cracking, Crashing, Glass]

Bubble: BOOOOOM, BOOMBOOP [see Balloon, Bouncing, Bubble, Liquid, Soup, Popping, Spring]
Bull see Animal
Bullet: BEOW, BLAMP, BOOM, BOOOMM, BRIT, BRITT, BWEEE, CHOK, DWEE, K-CHUNK, KING KONG, PAH, PANG, PING, PING PANG, PIUNG, POK, POOM, POOMF, POOMP, PTAK, PTANG, P-TANG, PWEE, SHTUP, SKREEOW, SPAK, SPANG, SPING, SPLANG, SPLAT, SPRANG-WAH, SPRUK, SPUKK, SPWANG, SPWE, SPWEE, STOK, THWIP, TING, TOK, TWEEN, TWING, TZING, TZNG, VING, VIP, ZIP, ZING, ZZHIP [see Gun, Ricochet, Weapon]
Burning: FFFFSST, FSHSSSTTT, FWROOSH, FZZZT, FZZZZT, POOF, SHZZZZT, SIZZLE, SIZZLE SITZ, SPOOF, SSSSSSSST, SSSSSSTTTT, SSZZHH, VROOSHH [see Flint]
Burping see Belching
Buzzing: BBZZTTT, BBZZZTT, BUZZ, BUZZZ, BZZT, BZZZ, BZZZZ, BZZZZZZ [see Alarm, Bell, Horn, Indicator, Signal, Siren, Radar, Telephone]
Card: FERRIP, FLIK
Cat see Animal
Chain: CHING, CHINGG, CHINKCHKCHAKK, CHUKK [see Mechanical, Metal, Noise]
Chainsaw: BZZARR, BZZOOORRRR, BZZZZZTT, Chinkcnk Chakk [see Axe, Blade, Chain, Saw, Weapon]
Chalk: SKREEEEEEE
Chamelion see Animal
Chewing: CHEEEEEYEW, CHEEEEYEW, CHEWWA [see Eating, Drinking, Swallowing]
Children's sayings: NYAH, WHEEEEEEE, ZOWIE [see Exclamations]
Clock: TICK, TOCK, TRANG TRANG [see Alarm]
Coin: CLINK, FLADIP, FPP, KLINK GLINK, KLINKADINK, PLINK, plink, TAK
Cold: BURR, FROOOOSH, FROOSH
Clubbing: KRAK, NOKK, SMAKK, THUD, TONK, TUNGK, WHAPP [see Breaking, Crashing, Hitting, Weapon]
Collision: BA-BAMM, BASH, BLAM, BOP, BRAM, BUMP, CRASH, CRASHH, CRUNCH, FA-WHUMP, FAH-BHAMMM, FAK, FOOM, FUPP, GLABADAP, GONK, KA-CHOOM, KA-ROOOOOSH, KA-THRASH, KATCHOOM, KATRANG, KLANG, KRANCH, KRARASH, KRNCH, KTHUNK, KUMP, KWAM, MABBIT, SPAMAMP, SPLATT, THUGAWUNK, WHAM, WHAMB, WHAMM, WHUMP, WOM [see Crashing, Hitting, Explosions]

Contempt: HMMMMPH [see Raspberry, Symbols]
Cooing: OOOOO, OOOOOO [see Kissing, Love, Pleasure]
Coughing: GAHAK, KAFF, KAFF-KAFF, KAHAK, KAHIKE, KAPF, KIFF, KOFF [see Sneezing]
Cracking: CRACK, KKKK, KRAKK, KRRIK [see Breaking, Crunching]
Crashing: CAR-RAM, CHASH, CRASH, CRASHH, CRSHK, KARASH, KARASHH, KASHH, KEE-RASH, KERAASH, KLASHT, KRAAASH, KRARASH, KRASH, K-RASH, KRESHH, SKRASH, SHRASHH, SKRASHH, SKRASSH, SKRAZH, SPA-KRASHH [see Collision]
Cries of pain, suffering, terror, rage, fear etc.: AAAA, AAAAA, AAAAAAA, AAAAAAAAA, AAAAAAAGHHH, AAAAAAAHHHHHHH, AAAAGGHH, AAAAGH, AAAAHH, AAAARGH, AAAARRRGH, AAAARRRR, AAAG, AAAGG, AAAGGGH, AAAGGGK, AAAGGK, AAAIIEEE, AAAKHH, AAARGH, AAARGHHH, AAIIEEEE, AAIIIEEEEE, AARGH, AARRGH, ARRHH, ARRGGGGG, AARRRRR, AGGAAAAAA, AGHA, AGHH, AGHHH, AGHHHHHH, AGK, AHH, AHHH, AHHHHHGH, AIEGHH, AKKK, AKKKK, ARGGH, ARRGHH, ARRGHHH, ARRHH, ARRRRRR, EEE-EE-EE, EEEYOWW, EEYAAA, EEYAGH, EEYARGH, EEYARGX, GAA, GARR, GRAAH, HNNNGNN, KHAKK, OOFPH, OW, OWW, OWWW, OWWWW, UGKH, UNNHH, UNNNGHH, UNNNH, UUUUURP, UUUUUUUUUUUUNNN, YAA, YAAA, YAAAAA, YAAAAAAGH, YAAG, YAGGGGHHHHHHHH, YEE-OUCH, YEEAAGK, YEEARGH, YEEEAAAHR, YEEEARGH, YEEOOW, YEOW, YOW, YYYAAHHAAAGGHH, YYYY
Crying: OOOOOO, SOB [see Cries, Moaning, Wailing]
Crunching: KAA-RUUNNCH, KEE-RUNCH, KR-RUNCH, KRANCH, KRUNK, KU-RONNCH, RRUNCHT, SCRNCH, SKRUNCH, THRUNCH [see Breaking, Cracking]
Cutting: BLEUGHZ, CLIP, SHAKKKT, SHUNK, SKLORPSKX, SLSSHH, SNIK, SNIKK, SWASHHH, THOIP, THWOK, VZZZT, VZZZZT, VZZZZZZZZZZZT, ZLIKT [see Axe, Blade, Chainsaw, Saw, Slashing]
Dieing: ACK-YAK, AGGH, ARGH, AWK, BLBBL FLB BLBBPLP, GAK, GASP, HAK-GASP, HUKK, YAF-SLISH [see Morgue]
Diving: PLOUF [see Liquid, Water]
Dog see Animal
Door: BAM, BRAKK, BTHWAKKT, CRASH, FAM, KER-BASH, KNOCK, KRAK, KUKK, NOK, NOKK, NOK NOK,

SLAM, SLLANK, SSSSHHHHHH, TAP, TOK, WHACK, WHAM, WHUMP, WOMP [see Slamming]
Drill, pneumatic: RATA..TATA..TA..TA
Drinking: GLiT, GLUK, SLERP, SLURP [see Chewing, Eating, Soup]
Eating: BLATCH, BLECCH, CHEWWA, CHEEEEYEW, CHEEEEEYEW, CHOMP, CHOMPLE, GLOMP, GLUK, GLUMP, GULP, KADOONK, KRUNK, MMMMM, MMMMMM, MUNCH, ORG, SCARF, SLURP, Slurp...crunch..., SPLORK, ULP, YUM [see Chewing, Drinking, Soup]
Electric eel see Animal
Electronic & Electrical: BRRZZT, CHCHASH, CHOOM, FFRZZAAK, FZZASH, FZZZRATCH, FZZZZL, GZZZT, KAZAK, KKKKRRRRAAAAAKKKKKLLLL, KKKRAKKKKLL, KRAKKKL, KRAKKL, KRAKKLL, KRRAKKLLL, KZAKK, KZAT, KZZZAT, PRZZAT, RRZZTTT, SHZZZZT, SVASH, SZIT, TZZZZTT, ZAPT, ZRASH, ZZRAAK, ZZRAK, ZZRAKK, ZZRAKSH, ZZRARKT, ZZRRAKKK, ZZWWAKT, ZZZRAKK, ZZZRATCH, ZZZT, ZZZWAKK [see Energy, Radio, Switch]
Energy: BAZAKK, BRRRZZZZZAP, BRRZZT, BZZAPP, CHCHASH, CHOOM, CHOOMSKH, CRA....KWOOOM, CRZZPT, DEET, FAASSH, FACHOW, FASH, FAZ, FFRZZAAK, FLAMM, FLASH, FOOSH, FRAAK, FROOOSH, fSHOOM, f-SHOOOOOOM, FTHOOM, FWATHOOM, FWOOM, FWOOOM, FWOOSH, FWOOOOSHH, FWOOOSH, FZZAKKL, FZZASH, FZZT, FZZZRATCH, FZZZT, FZZZZT, FZZZZ, FZZZZL, FZZZZZ, FZZZZZZZZ, GZZZT, KATOOOSH, KAZAK, KKKKRRRRAAAAAKKKKKLLLL, KKKRAKKKLL, KRACK, KRAACK, KRA-ACK, KRAK, KRAKC, KRAKA DOOM, KRAKKL, KRAKKKL, KRAKKLL, KRAKKLE, KRAKOW, KRRAKKLLL, KZAKK, KZAT, KZZZAT, PRZZAT, PTOOM, RRZZTTT, SHAK, SHAZZAP, SHOOM, SHOOW, SHRACK, SHRAKAKAKA KAKAKAKA, SHRAKK, SHRAKOOM, SHRAZZAK, SHRING, SHTOOOOOOOOOM, SHYEK, SHYMMMMSS, SHZZTHSSSSSSSSSS, SHZZZZT, SKOOMPH, SKRAZAK, SPTAK, SRREE, SVASH, SVBEEP, SWOOSH, SZHKK, SZIT, THRAKAKAKAKAKA, THWAAASHHH, TZAPT, TZZZZTT, VREE, VREEEEEEEEEEEE, VREEEEEEEEEEEEEEET, VREEEET, VREET, VREEEEEE, WHREEEP, WHREEP, WREEEP, ZAP, ZAPOW, ZAPPP, ZAPPPPPPP, ZAPT, ZOAM, ZPFT, ZVIPT, ZRAAK, ZRAK, ZRASH, ZVVPPTTTT, ZZAM, ZZCHATHZZ, ZZRAAK, ZZRAK,

ZZRAKK, ZZRARKT, ZZRRAKKK, ZZWAKKT, ZZWAKK,
ZZRAKSH, ZZRAP, ZZRARKT, ZZRRAKKK, ZWAKKT,
ZZZCHATHZZZ, ZZZOTZH, ZZZRAKK, ZZZRATCH, ZZZT,
ZZZWAKK, ZZZZT, ZZZZTHSHYEEK, ZZZZZT [see
Electronic]
Exclamations, Interjections: $#!*, @$$#*!#, AAAARGH,
AAARGH, AAAARGH, AAARGH, AAAARGH, AAHH,
AGOOOOOGAH, AH-HAH, AH, AHA, AHHH, AHHHHHH,
ARRARGH, ARRRRGH, BAH, BAWWWW, BLA, BLABBLA,
BLEAH, BLIP, BULL#$%¢&*!, D'OH , DWAT, EEE-YUK,
EEE, EEEEEEEEEE, EEEEEEEEEEEEE also
EEEEEEEEEEEEEEE also EEEEEEEEEEEEEEEEEEE,
EEEE-EE-EEE-EE, EE-EEE-EEEE-EE, EEEUW, EEEYOWW,
EEYAAA, EEYAGH, EEK, EEEK, EEP, FITZROWER, HEY-
YY, HHUYECHH, HMMM, HMMMM, Hmmmmm...,
HMMMMM..., HMMMMPH, HNH?, HOORAY, hrn?, I-YI-YI,
JEEZ, KIDDO, Mmm-Hmm, MMM, MMMM, MMMMMMM,
Mmmm hmmm, MMMMPH, NAAAH, NAAAAH, NAW,
NOOOO, NOOOOOO, NO-O-O-O-O, NYAH, OH, OH-OH,
OHH, OMIGOD, oohhhhh, OOO, OOOH, OOOOO, OOOOOO,
OOO...OOO...OO, OOOPS, OO-OOPS, Ooooops..., OOOOPS,
OUTTA, PHEW, RAH, RRRAAARRRR, RRRRRRR,
SHADDAP, SHHHHH, SHRIEK, THHRRRP, UM,HMMM,
UNH, URK, URPH, UUNNNH..., UUURRRGGGHH, WAA,
WHEEEEEEE, WHOOPEE, WOOWOOWOOWOO, YA-A-A,
YAAAAA, YAAAAAAAAHHH, YAYAYAHHH,
YAYAYAYAYAHHH, YAAAHH, YAAAIIIEEEE, YAAH,
YAHOO, YAK, Yecccch, YECCCH, YECCH, YEE-HA, YEE-
HAW, YEH, YIII, YIIII, YIIKES, YIPPY, YOO HOO,
ZOWIE, ! [see Children's Sayings, Symbols]
Explosion: BA-DOOM, BA-DOOOMM, BA-DOOOMMM, BA-
R-RA-ROOM, BAA-ROOM, BAAA-ROOMM,
BAAAROOOOM, BAAA-DOOOW, BADABOOM,
BADABOOOM, BAM, BAROOM, BARROOM, BARROOOM,
BBBARRROOOMM, BHWOOOM , BLA-DROOOM, BLAH-
DA BOOOOOM, BLA-AAAAMMM, BLA-AAAAM, BLAM,
BLAAM, BLAAMMM, BLAM BLAM, BLAMM, BLAST,
BLOOSH, BOOM, BOOM-KA-BOOM, BOOMM, BOOOM,
BOOOMM, BOOOOM, BOOOOOM, BRA-KOOOM,
BRAAAAM, BTOOOM, BUDOOOM, BUH-BOOM, BWOOM,
BWOOOOM, BWOOOOOM, CHOOM, CHOOMSKH,
CROOOM, DOOM, FLOON, FOOOM, FTOOM, FUH-
WHOOM, FUMP, FWAKOOM, FWOOM, FWZAAM, K-POW,
KaBOOM, KA-BOOM, KA-BOOOM, KA-BOOOMM, KA-
BOOOMMMM, KA-BOOOOM, KADOOOM, KAPOWW, K-

POWW, KA-RUMP, KA-WHOOOM, KA CHOOM, KA-CHOOM, KA POKK, KA-POKK, KA-POKK!POKK, KABLOOM, KADOOM, KATOOOM, KRA DA BOOM, KRAKADOOM, KRAKATOWWW, KRAKOOOOM, KROOM, LEBOOM, MOWM, PAF, PAROOM, PCHOOM, PHROOOM, POOM, POOMF, POOMP, POP, POWW, PTHOOOM, PTOOM, PWAKA-PWOOM, SHAAKKOW, ShaKOOM, SHH-FOOM, SHRABOOM, SHRACKKKKKK, SKA-KOOM, SKOOM, SKRA-KABOOM, SSHHFFOOOOOSH, SSSHHABA-BOOOOM, SSSSSSSSSSSSSHBLAMM, SWATHZZZWHOUMM, THKAM, THOOM, THWOOOM, THWRAKKAPWOMM, VOOM, WHAM, WHAMB, WHAMM, WHOMP, WHOOM [see Bullet, Energy, Gun, Laxative, Missile, Mortar, Thunder, Volcano, Weapon]

Falling: AAAA, AAAAA, AIEE, BLONK, CHOK, CLUNK, CRASH, CRAASH, EEE-EE-EE, F-LOP, FLOON, FUMP, K-KLAKT, KAA-WHUUMPH, KAWHUMP, KEKK, KIT-TOONG, KLAK, KLLIMP, KLONNK, KLUD, KLUNK, KRA TAKKA TAKKA TAKKA TAM, KRRUMP, KRUUK, KSSHFWOOM, PLOP, PLOUF, POK, SHLOMP, SKWAPPO, SPLAT, THAK, THAKT, THUD, THUDD, THUMK, THUMP, THWOCK, WAP, WHUK, WHUKK, WHUMF, WUMP, WUMPP, YA-A-A, YAAAAA, YAAAIIEEEE [see Crashing, Rolling]

Farting: FRAP [see Body, Coughing, Farting, Laxative, Sneezing, Vomit]

Fear: AAAAAA, AAAAAAA, AAAAAAAAGHHHH, AAAAAAAAHHHHHHH, AAAHH, AAEEEK, AHHH, AHHHHHHHH, AIIEEE , AIIIIE, AKKK, ARGH, EEEEE, EEEEEEEE, EEEEEEEEEE, EEEEEEEEEEEE, EEEEEEEEEEEEEEE, EEEEEEEEEEEEEEEEEEE, EEEE-EE-EEE-EE, EE-EEE-EEEE-EE, EeeEEKK, EEEEK, GAAAH, HALLLPYAAAA, RRREEEEEEE, SCREECH, SCREEECH, SCREEE, SCREEEE, SCREEEEE, SCREEEEEEECHH, SKEEEE, SKEEEEE, SKREEE, SKREEEE, SKREEEEEEEE, SKREEL, SCREEECHHH, SCREEEECCHH, SCREEECH, SKREEE, SKREEEEE, SKREEEE, SKREEEEEEEE , skreek, YAAAHH, YEOW, YEEOOW, YEEOWWW [see Cries]

Flight: DWEE, FFF FFFT, FSSHH, FZOOOOOSH, OOOSSH, PHHHHHT, SHING, SHROOM, SHROOOOM, SWOOP, VA-THROOOOM, VOOSH, VOOOSH, VROOSH, VRUUM, VSSHHHH, VVVVVSSSSSS, VZZZT, VZZZZT, VZZZZZZZZZZZT, WHEEEE, ZZVT [see Missile, Space Ship, Speeding]

Flint: SHIKA-SHIKA, ZIK ZIK ZIK

Footstep: BOOM, DUNT, HEP, KLIK KLAK, PADAP, PITTER-PAT, STOMPUH, STOOM, TROMP

Frog see Animal

Glass: BLASHH, BOSH, BREEESH, CRACK, CRASH, KASHH, KEE-RASH, KERAASH, KEERASSH, KER-SMASHH, KHRASSH, KKKSH, KKKSSH, KRA-TINKLE, KRAKC, KRASH, KRASHH, KRESHH, KRISSH, KRRAASSSHH, KSSSHHHH, KTAAASHHH, SKA-RASHH, SKLANG, SKRASH, SKRIKSH, SMASH, SPA-KRASHH, TINKLE, TINKLE TINK INK [see Break, Crash]

Groaning: ERGHHH, GEHHHH, UHHNNNNN..., UNNGHH, UNNHH, UNNNGHHH..., UUHH, UUUUUUUUUUUUUNNN... [see Cries, Crying, Moaning, Wailing]

Growling: AARRGH, ARRGH, Arrrgh, GGGRRRR, GROWL..., GRRARR, GRRR, GRR, GRRR..., GRRRR, GRRRR..., GRRRRRR..., GRRRRRR, GRR..., GRRRRRRRR, GRRRR, GR-R-R-R, GRRRRR, ROARRRR, ROARL, RROARR, RRRG [see Roaring, War cry]

Grunting: AGH, ARG, EEEEYAAAAH, GGGRRR, GGGRRRAAA, HHEYUUHHHH, HHHRURRR, HNNN, MMMPPPHHHHH, MMMWWWAAA, MMMWWWUUHH, NFF, NNGHHH, RRRRAAAAAAA, UGH, UHNNFF, UNNGHH, UNG, UNGH, UNNGH, UNH, UNPH [see Physical exertion]

Guns: BAM, BAMM, BANG, BDAM, BLA-DRAMM, BLAM, BLA-AAAAM, BLAAM, BLAAMMM, BLAMM, BLAM BLAM, BLAMBLAM, BLAMM, BOOM, BOOOMM, BRAK, BRAKA, BRAKABRAKABRAKA, BRAP, BRAAP, BRAAAP, BRATATAT, BRAT A TAT A TAT, BRAT-A-TAT-TAT, BRATCH, BRRA-A-A-AP, BRRRAP, BRRRAPP, BRRRAAAP, BRRRR, BRRRRP, BUDA, BUDDA, BUDDABUDDA, BUDDAB, BUDDURP, BUHBOOM, BWOOM, BWOOOOM, BWOOOOOM, CHA-CHUNK, CHA-POW POW, CHAKKA, CHAM, CHAT-CHOOM, CHOOM, CHOOMSKH, CHOW, CHPOW, CLICK, FFFT, FOOM, FUP, FUPP, KA-BAM, KAPOW, KAPOWW, KATOOF, KLIK, KPOW, KRAK, KRACK KRACK, KTOW, PAN, POOM, POOMP, POW, PUNCH, RATATAT, RATATATAT, RATATATATA, RATATATATAT, RATATATATATA, RATATATATATAT, RATATATATATATA, RAT-TA-TA-TA, RAT-TA-TAT, RAT-TAT, RAT-TAT-TAT, RATA-TATTATTATTAT, RATATATATATATAT, SHAAKKOW, SHK-SHKT, SPAK, TATTTA, WHAMM, WHRRRRR-TCHAK, ZARCH, ZHARCH,

ZKRAT, ZRAKT, ZWAZASH, ZZAT [see Bullet, Ricochet, Weapon]

Gurgling: ERGHHH, GLAGGG, GLUG, GURGG, GURGLE, RRGL, URRGL [see Bubble, Liquid, Slop, Slurp, Soup, Toxic Waste, Water]

Hitting: BA-TANG, BAM, BAP, BAPP, BDOW, BIFF, BLAM, BLANG, BLIKX, BMPH, BOK, BONK, BOOM, BOP, BRACK, BRAKK, BROK, BTAM, BTOK, BWAK, BWAKT, BWAM, BWOOOOOM, BWOP, BWUMPT, CHAK, CHOK, CHOMP, CHOP, CHUDD, CHUK, CLONG, CLONK, CLOP, CLOPS, CONK, CRACK, CRAACK, CRAAKK, CRASH, CRUMP, CRUNCH, CRUNNCHHH, DIT, DOINK, DUNT, FAK, FAP, FAPP, FFFT, FLANG, FLOON, FRUNK, FTHOOM, FWOOM, FWUD, FUD, FWA-BOK, FWACKT, FWAK, FWAP, FWIBTHH, FWUD, GDONG, GLING, K-BAM, KA-DOONK, KA ROOOOM, KABASH, KABLOOM, KACHONK, KAPOW, KAPTHOOM, KEKK, KEE-RUNCH, KER-BASH, KLANK, KLOMP, KLONK, KLONNK, KLOON, KLOONK, KLOOONN, KLUD, KLUDD, KLUGG, KLUNK, KRACK, KRAACK, KRA-ACK, KRAAK, KRAK, KRAKK, KRAM, KREESH, KROOOM, KRUNTCH, KTHUMP, KUGG, KUH-WANG, KUKK, KUNK, KWAM, KWAMM, KWONG, KWOOOOMP, NOK, NOK NOK, OOOOF, PAFF, PAH, PHAK, PHOOK, PHTOOP, PHTOW, PLAFF, PLOW, POINK, PONG, POOM, POP, POT, POW, PTHUMP, PTOK, PTOW, PWOOM, SHAAKKOW, SHA-BLAM, SHAK, SHARAK, SHCHUKK, SHLOMP, SHMAMP, SHRACKKKK, SHRAK, SHRAKK, SHUK, SHUMM, SHUNK, SHVRAM, SHWAK, SHWAM, SKAPOW, SKRUKK, SLAM, SLAMM, SLAP, SLAPITY SLAP, SLAPITY SLAP SLAP, SLOK, SMACK, SMAK, SMAKK, SMEK, SOCK, SOK, SPAK, SPING, SPKANNG, SPLAATT, SPLAAATTTT, SPLAK, SPLANG, SPLAT, SPLATT, SPLATTT, SRRAK, STOONG, SWACK-K-K, SWAT, SWIF, SWOK, SWUMP, TCHOC, THCHTH, TCHUNK, THAKOMPH, THAMM, THOK, THOMP, THONGK, THOP, THUD, THUDD, THUK, THUMP, THUNK, THWACK, THWAK, THWAMM, THWOKK, TOCK, TOK, TONG, TONK, TOOM, TUNGK, TUNK, UMMPH, UNGGG, UNGH, UNNGH, UNPH, WAK, WHAM, WHANG, WHAP, WHAPP, WHAPPP, WHOMP, WHOOOMMMM, WHUD, WHUDWHUD, WHUK, WHUKK, WHUMP, WHUNK, WOK, WOM, WOMO, WROK, WUD, WUMF, ZAPT, ZRASH, ZZRASH, ZZZINK, ZZZRATCH, ZZZZINK [see Kicking]

Horn: AAH-OOOH-GAH, AGOOOOOGAH, AOOG, AOOGAOOGAOO, AROOGA, AROOGAH,

AROOGAHAROOGAH, BEEP, BEEEP, BEEEEP, BEEEEEP, BLAT BLAT, HONK! HONK!, OOOO: [see Alarm, Buzzing, Car, Indicator, Motorcycle, Signal, Siren]
Horror see Cries
Horse see Animal
Ghost: AWROOOO, BOO, EEEAGGHHHH
Ignition: CLIK, FFZT, GNAA [see Car, Mechanical, Motorcycle]
Indicator: BEEP, DINGG [see Alarm, Bell, Buzzing, Horn, Indicator, Signal, Siren, Radar, Telephone]
Insect see Animal
Kicking: BAM, BAPP, BDOK, BLUNNT, BRAK, BRAKT, CHUD, CLONK, CLOP, CRACK, CRASH, FWAK, FWUMP, HWOKSH, KAKK, KLANGK, KLONK, KLOOM, KLUD, KRAK, KRAKK, KRESH, KRUKK, KRUMP, KUD, KUDD, KUKK, SCHWOK, SKUP, SKWAKO, SMACK, SPANG, THHUD, THOMP, THUDUD, THUMP, THUNK, THWUK, WHAP, WHAPPWHUK, WHUMP, WRAKT, WUMP, WUNK [see Hitting]
Kissing see Cooing, Love, Pleasure
Knocking: KLOP, KNOCK, NOK, POT, TOK [see Hitting, Tapping]
Landing: KLLIMP, SPLITCH, THUMP, WHAM, WHAPP, WHUMF, WOM, WUMPP [see Collision, Falling]
Laughter: BWA-HA-HA-HA, CHOKE, CHUCKLE, GAG, HA, HAAAHAAA, HA HA, HAH, HAR, HAHAHAHAHA, HA HA HAHO HA HOOT HOO HA HA, HA-HA, HA HA HA HA HA HA, HA-HAHAHA, HAHAHA, HAHA, HAR, HEE-HEE, HEE, HEEEEEEEEE, HEH-HEH, HEH-HEH-HEH-HEH-HEH, HEHEHEHE, HEHEHEHEHE, HO, HO HO HA HA HEE HO, HOO-HA HA HA HA HA HA, HOO, HOO HAA, HYUK, NYA HA HA, TEE, HEE [see Pleasure]
Lawn mower: WHIR WHIR
Laxative: BOOMER-ROOM
Liquid: BLBBL FLB BLBBPLP, BLOOSH, BLOP, BLORP, BLORSH, BLUB, BOOMBOOP, FERSPLASH, FIZZ, FLSSH, FSSSIP, FZSSSSSSSSS, GAPLORK, GLAGGG, GLOOP, GLORP, GLUB, GLUG-GLUG, GLUG, GLUP, GURGLE, GURGG, KER-PLASH, KER-splash, PLASH, PLOIPLE, PLOPLE, PLOOPPLOOPPLOOP, PLOP, PLORP, PLUNK, PLURP, SHKLAP, SHKLIZORTCH, SHKSHH, SHLORP, SKLOOSH, SLOP, SPA-BASH, SPAZOOSH, SPLASH, SPLASHH, SPLASHLE, SPLAT, SPLAZOOSH, SPLOOSH, SPLOSH, SPLUBLE, SSSHLORP, SSSSSSSHHHH, URRGG,

VROOM SPOOSH see Bubble, Gurgling, Slopping, Soup, Slurping, Swallowing, Toxic Waste, Water]
Lock: KLAKK, KLICK, TCHIKT, UNKLIK, ZWIT [see Mechanical, Metal]
Love: ARRARGH, BLAMP, BOING, SMACK, MFFFF..., MMMMMMM, MMMMMMMMMMMMMM, OOF, OOO, OOOH, OOOOO, OOOOOO, OOOO, OOOOO, OOOOOO, OOOOOOO, SMACK, UHMMMM, UNNH, WAMP, YUG [see Cooing, Kissing, Pleasure]
Magic: FFFT, FWOOM, POP, SHA-ZAM, SHAZ...HIC, VRZMMVRZMM [see Energy, Popping]
Martial Arts: AAIIEEEE, AAIIIEEEEE, CHUK, HAAAAR, HAIII, HAYYY YAHH, HII-YAAAH, KONK, KRAKK, KUKK, KUNK, THONK, ZONK [see Cries]
Mechanical: BANG, BLAP, BRDAP, CHAK, CHIK, CHIKKT, CHTTHZZ, CHUNK, CLACK, CLANG, CLANK, CLICK, CLIKK, CLONK, CRANK, CREAAK, CREEAK, CREEEEK, FEEP, FIZZ, FZZ, GROON, K-K-KREAK, KA-SPANG, KACHUNK, KLACK, KLAK, KLICK, KLAKATA-KLAKATA, KLANG, KLANKT, KLIK-GROOON, KLIK, KLIKITA-KLKITA, KLOP, KLUNK, KNOCK, KNOK, KREEE, KREEK, POIT, POP, PRUKT, RAP, RYENK, SCHPLOOK, SHKREEUUHHHH, SHOOP, SKREEK, SKRRR, SKWEEK, SNAKT, SNAP, SPANG, SPLANG, SWISH, TAK, TCHAKK, TCHIKT, tinnng, TTZZ, WHIRRR, WHIRRRRRRRR, ZIP, ZZT, ZZTZZT, ZZZT, ZZZZZZTZZZTZZZ [see Chain, Lock, Metal, Noise]
Metal: CLANK, KLANK, KTANGG, SLLANK, SPANG [see Chain, Lock, Mechanical]
Missile: CHOONT, PFFHT, SHROOM, SHROOOOM, SSHUK, VA-THROOOOM, VOOOSH [see Flight, Weapon]
Moaning: UUNNNH... [see Cries, Crying, Groaning, Wailing]
Morgue: FAGROOLANA, FASHUNK
Morphing: ARRGH, BEEYOOP, GARRGH, SLORPH
Mortar: BLAM: WHEEEE [see Weapon]
Motor: BBBDROOM, BRAAAAWN, BRRAAOOOM, ROARRRR, RROOAARR, VROOM, VROOOM, WHIR, WHIRRRR, WHIRRRRRRRR [see Car, Horn, Ignition, Mechanical, Motorcycle]
Motorcycle: BRAAAAOWN, BRRAAOOOM, RROOAAARR [see Horn, Ignition, Motor]
Music: BANG CRASH, BANG CRASH BOOM, Bap-de-bow..., BOM, BOOM, BRMMMMMMMMMMMMMMMMMMM, BUH-BA-BA-BA-BUHM, DUM-TI-DUM, FEEOOOT, iFFFFPFP, RATTATATTAT, RUB-A-DUB DUB-A-DUB A-DUB,

Shoo-be-doo, shoo-boo...dah-be-dah, TA, TAA, TAAA,
TAAAAA, TA TA TA TA, TAA-DAAA, TATARRA TARRA
TARRA, TOOB, TWEEP, Zap...pow
Noise, background: BATANG, BOOM, BOOM-KA-BOOM,
BOOMM, BOOOMM, BOOOOM, BOOOOOM, CLANG,
COOM, DASH, DOON, FASHOOM, FOOM, GASHLIKT,
GLOOCHLE, GWARRR, HURRRRR, KARASHBOOMBAM,
KASH, KKKRRRROOOMM, KRUNCH KRINKLE KRINKLE
KRITCH, RAAARR, RAKKKT, RAUGHHHHHH,
RRRRUMMMMBLLE, RRRUMMBLLE,
RRRRRRRMMMMMMMMMMBBLL, RUMMMMMM, SHIK,
SHKLOORT, SHOOP, SKLUTCH, SKREEEEEEEE, SPLITCH,
SPLOTCH, SPMAMP, SPWAP, SQULRRCH, TANG,
THLOOP, THUNK, THURCH, VWAP GAA-RIEP VROOM,
WHRRRR
Pain: AAAA, AAAAA, AAAAAA, AAAAAAAAA,
AAAAGGHH, AAAAARGH, AAAAGGH, AAAARRRRGH,
AAAARRRGHHH, AAAARRRRR, AAAG, AAAGG,
AAAGGGH, AAAGGK, AAAHH, AAAHHRR, AAAIIEEE,
AAAK, AAAAK, AAAKHH, AAARGHHH, AARGH, AARRH,
AARRHH, AARRGGGGG, AARRRRR, AGHHHHHHH,
AGHA, AGHH, AGHHH, AGHHHHHH, AGH-K, AIEGHH,
AKKKK, AOWW, ARGGH, ARRGHH, ARRGHHH,
ARRRGHHH, ARRRRRR, AAAAAAA--*, AGK, AEEEE,
AGGGH, AIIEEE, AIIIIE, ARRRGH, EEEE, EEEECCCHH,
EEEYOWW, EEYAAA, EEYAGH, EEYARGH, EEYARGX,
GAA, GAKKK, GARR, GEHHHH, GYAAAARHHH,
HNNNGNN, KHAKK, KRUNK, NAAAAA, NNNNNNNG,
OOOOF, OOFPH, OOOUUUCHHH, OUCH, OW, OOWW,
OWWW, OWWWW, OWWWWWWW, REEEE, SKREEE,
SKREEEEE, SKREEEE, SKREEEEEEEE, UFFT, UGKH,
UNNNGHH, UNNNH, URRUGH, UUUUURP, YAA,
YAAAAAAGH, YAAG, YAGGGGHHHHHHHH, YAAAGH,
YEE-OUCH, YEOW, YOW, YEEOOW, YEEOWWW,
YEOWWWWW, YYYAAHHAAAGGHH, YYYY [see Cries]
Paint: SPLAT, SPLAZATCH, SPLAZITCH, SPLUT, SPLUTT,
SQUIRT, SQUISH
Physical Exertion: EEEEYAAAAH, GGGRRRRAAA,
GGGRRRR, HHEYUUHHHH, HHHRURRR,
MMMPPPHHHHH, MMMWWAAA, MMMWWWUUHH,
NNGHHH, RRRRAAAAAAA [see Groaning, Grunting]
Phone see Telephone
Pipe: BLANG, CLONG, GDONG see Hitting, Metal]
Pleasure: AHHH, OOOO, YAHOO, ZOWIE [see Cooing,
Kissing, Love, Laughter]

Popping: BLEEP, BLOIT, BOIING
Punching: BAM, BLIKX, BWAK, CHAK, CHOK, CHOP, CHUDD, CHUK, CLOPS, CRACK, CRUNCH, CRUNNCHHH, FAPP, FUD, KAPTHOOM, KRAAK, KREESH, KUGG, KUH-WANG, PAFF, PHOOK, PLAFF, POK, POW, PTOW, SHUK, SKAPOW, SMACK, SMECK, SOCK, SPLAAATTTT, SPLAATT, SPLANG, SPLATTT, SWUMP, TCHOC, THONGK, THUD, THUK, THWAK, THWAMM, THWOKK, TOCK, WHANG, WHUDD, WHUDDWHUDD, WHUK , WOK, WOM, WROK, WUD [see Hitting, Kicking]
Radar: BEEP [see Alarm, Electronic, Indicator, Radio, Signal]
Radio: CRRR, TRIII, TRIIIUUW, WOOUUIIIII, ZEEZEE: [see Electronic, Radar, Signal, TV]
Rage see Cries
Rat see Animal
Ricochet: PING, SPANG, TZING [see Bullet, Gun, Weapon]
Roaring: GWARRR, RAAARR, ROARRRR, RROOAAARR, RRRRAARGH [see Growling, War cry]
Rolling: BROUM, BROUMMM, BRROUUMM, FLAPTAPTAP, KRASH, ROLL, RRRMMMBBLLL, ZZZZZZIZZZZ [see Falling]
Rude: THHRRRP: see Symbol
Rushing: FWHEEEEE, FWOOSH, SHOOOM, SSSHOOOPPOOFF, SSSSSSSSSSWOSHH, VOOSH, VROOOSH, WOOOSH, ZWOOSH [see Speeding]
Saw: GRRRRRR, WRRZZ, ZANNNNNG [see Blade, Chainsaw, Cutting, Slicing]
Screaming: AHHHHHGH, EEEEEEEE, EEEEEEEEEEEEE, RRREEEEEEE, SCREEEEEE [see Cries, Crying, Moaning, Roaring, Wailing]
Sea serpent see Animal
Shaking: SHAKITYSHAKESHAKE, SHIKA, SHOOKA SHOOKA SHOOKA
Signal: BEEP, floof, FLOOF, floof floofity flif flif flof daflaf, TRIII, TRIIIUUW, WOOUUIIIII [see Alarm, Bell, Buzzing, Horn, Indicator, Radio, Signal, Siren, Radar, Telephone, TV]
Siren: EEEEEE, EEEEEEEEE, INGALINGALINGALINGALING, RRRRRR, WEEEEEE, WEEEOOOOWEEEOOOWEEEOOOO, WEEOOOOWEEEOOOOWEEE, WEEOOOWEEE, WEEOOOWEEEOOOOWEEEOOOO, WHOOPWHOOP, WHOOPWHOOPWHOOPWHOOPWHO, WOO-WOO-WOOO [see Alarm, Bell, Buzzing, Horn, Indicator, Signal, Radar]

Slamming: BLAT, BWUMPT, CHA-BAMM, CRASH, KRUNTCH, KWUFF, SKRAAM, THCHTH, THOOM, THUDOOM, THWAMM, WHAM, WUMF
Slapping: SLAPITYSLAPSLAP, SPLAT, WAK, WHAP [see Hitting]
Slashing: PRAYKKK, SWASHHH [see Cutting]
Sleeping see Snoring
Sliding: SSSSHHHHHH, SSSSSS
Slopping: BLORP, SLOP [see Gurgling, Liquid, Slurping, Soup, Toxic Waste, Water]
Slurping: SHLORP, SSSHLOR [see Gurgling, Liquid, Slopping, Soup, Toxic Waste, Water]
Smashing: FUPP, K-BAM [see Collision, Hitting]
Snapping: KLIK, SNAK, SNAP, THLIK [see Breaking]
Sneezing: A-A-ACHOO, AACHOOOOO [see Coughing]
Snoring / Sleeping: NNN NNN, Z, ZERK, ZERKK, ZURK, ZZ, ZZZ, ZZZZ, ZZZZ..., ZZZZZ, ZZZZZZ, ZZZZZZZ, ZZZZZZZZ
Soup: GAPLORK, GLIP, GLIT, GLOOP, PLIPPLE, PLOBBLE, SHLIPP, SHLOOP, SHLURP, SHPIKKLE, SKLOP, SLOTCH, slrrrk, SPLOP [see Eating, Gurgling, Liquid, Slopping, Water]
Space Ships: VROOOSH, VRUUM, VVVVVSSSSSS, WHOOSH [see Air Vehicle, Flight, Speed]
Special Mention: BLEUGHZ, BOOMER-ROOM, GRRRGUK, HACK-GACK-IKLE-SHLIK, PLORTCH, POINK, RRGL, SHKILITZ, SHOOSH, SKLAZONCHO, SKLORPSKX, SPLORP, SSZZHH, VLURSH
Speed: FFZT, FSSHH, FWIP, FWISK, FWISKITTY FWASK, FWOOSH, FWOOOSH, FWOOOOSH, FZOOOOOSH, KA-ROOOOOSH, KCHOOM, OOOSSH, PFFHT, PHHHHHHT, PHHHHHT, RRRRRRRRRRRRRRROOOOSSSHH, SHFFF, SHOOOM, SHROOM, SHROOOOM, SSSSSSSSSSWOSHH, SWAP, SWOOOOP, TOOM, VAA-ROOOMM, VARHOOOOMM, VAROOMMM, VAROOM ROWM, VOOMAROOMA, VOOSH also VOOOSH, VOOOOSH, VOWM, VROOM, VROOOOMM, VROOM SPOOSH, VROOSH, VROOOSH, VSSHHHH, WHEEEEEEE, WHIZZ, WHIZZZ, WHOOSH, WOOOSH, ZOOM, ZOOOOOMM, ZOOOSHHH, ZWOOSH [see Car, Flight, Missile, Motorcycle, Space Ship]
Splashing: FERSPLSHH, FLSSHH, KER-PLASH, SPLASH, SPLOSH [see Gurgling, Liquid, Slopping, Slurping, Soup, Toxic Waste, Water]
Spitting: PITOOIE, PTOO, PTOOEY

Spraying: FIZZAZZIT, FSSSIP, FWOOSH, GASHKLITZKA, GASHLITZGA, PFFFT, PSSSH, SH-SHPRITZZZZ, SPLASHLE, SPRAY, SPRIZZITZ
Spring: DINK-DINK-DINK-DIN, FLADOINNG, FSHPLAP, GADANG, GADOING, GLOING, GOING, GEEN GEEN, GING, GING GING, GINK, GOING, KTANGG, POING, SPROING, SPROOOING [see Bouncing]
Startled see Cries
Stomach: RROARR [see Chewing, Eating]
Surprise see Cries
Swallowing: GLUMP [see Chewing, Eating, Liquid, Water]
Sweeping: FWACH, FWISK, FWISKITTY FWASK, FWIZZACH, SHAZZATZ, ZACHITTY, ZICH
Switch: CLICK, CRANK, FEEP, KLIK, KLIK-GROOON, PLIC-K, SNAP, THLIK, TIK [see Electronic, Indicator, Mechanical]
Symbols: @$$#*!#, $#!* [see Rude]
Tapping: RAPRAPRAP, TAP, TAP TAP, TOC [see Typing]
Tearing: RIIPP, RYENK
Telephone: BEEP, BREENG, BING BONG, BRINGG, BRIIIIIING, BRINNG, BRNNGT, BZZZ, EEP, FEEP, GEEP, GLEEP, GRING, RING, RINNG, RIN-NG, R-RING, RING-A-LING, RRING, RRING-A-LING-A-LING, RRRINNG, RRRING, RRRINNG, RRRRING, RRRRIINNNNGGG, SLAM, ZAZZIK, ZIK, ZIKKA, ZIZZAK [see Alarm, Bell, Buzzing, Indicator, Signal]
Television see TV
Terror see Cries
Thought: HMM, HMMMMM...
Throat: AHEM, AH-HEM, AHEM, ARRARGLE, HHUURGG, HUKK, RRGL [see Dieing, Exclamations]
Thunder: B-DAMM-D-D, KTAK KTAK BALOWM, BOOM [see Explosions]
Toxic waste: FIZZZ, GURGLE, PLOP, SPLOSH [see Bubble, Gurgling, Liquid, Slopping, Slurping, Water]
TV: BZZZZ, CLICK, ROWRRR, WHOOOOOOOOOOOOOOOOOOOOOOO [see Radio, Telephone]
Typing / Typewriter: TAKA TAKA TAK [see Tapping]
Vacuum cleaner: VROOM
Vehicle: BA-RROO-MM, BAHWAHHHH, BBBDROOM, BEEEEP, BEEEP, BLAT BLAT, BRAAAAOWN, BRRAAOOOM, CHUGGA CHUG CHUG CHUG, CLACKITY CLACK, CLICK, CRRUNCH, GNAA, HONK! HONK!, MMMBUH-WHAMMM, RINK-RIK, ROARRRR,

RROOAAARR, RRRRHUUUMMM, RRRRR, SCREEEECCHH,
SCREEEEEE, SCREEEEK, SKREEE, SKREEEEE, SKREEEE,
SKREEEEEEEE, SKREEEECH, SCREEEEEEECHH, SKREEL,
SPANG, SPUT-T SPUT-T CHUK-SPUT, THUMP THUMP,
VAA-ROOOMM, VAROOMMM, VAROOM ROWM,
VOOMAROOMA, VROOM, VROOOOMM, V-ROOOM [see
Ignition, Motor]
Volcano: BALLOOM, BOOM, RUMBLE
Vomit: BAAARRRRFFFF, BARF..., BLACCH [see Eating]
Wailing: EEEAGGHHHH, EEEEEEEEEE,
EEEEEEEEEEEEE, EEEEEEEEEEEEEEE,
EEEEEEEEEEEEEEEEEEE [see Cries, Crying, Groaning,
Moaning, Screaming]
War Cry: YAAAAAAAAHHH, YAYAYAHHH,
YAYAYAYAYAHHH [see Exclamations, Roaring]
Water: PLUNK, SHKSHH, SPLASH, SPLASHH,
SSSSSSSHHHH [see Gurgling, Liquid, Slopping, Slurping,
Soup, Toxic Waste]
Weapon: BAOOOM, BAOUM, BLAM, BLA-AAAAM,
BLAAM, BLAAMMM, BLAMM, BLAM BLAM, BLAMBLAM,
BLAMM, BLESHH, BOAM, BOAMM, BOOM, BOOM-KA-
BOOM, BOOMM, BOOOM, BOOOMM, BOOOOM, BrrrT,
BRRRTTT, BRRZZT, BZZAPP, CHCHASH, CHFF, CHOOM,
CHOOMSKH, CHOONT, CHUFF, CLOP, CRACK, CRAACK,
FOOM, FZZASH, FZZZRATCH, GZZZT, KACK, KCHOW,
KKRITCH, KLIK KLAK, KRACKLE, KRAKOW, KRIZZ,
KROOOOOSHHH, KWOOOOMP, KZAKK, KZAT, KZZZAT,
PHOONT, PLIK, PLOK, POOOOOF, PRZZAT,
RATATATATATAT, RRR-OOOOOSHH, RRZZTTT,
SFROOSH, SHAK, SHAZZAP, SHIIIIIIING, SHRAKOOM,
SHRAZZAK, SHRING, SHZZTHSSSSSSSSSS, SKRAZAK,
SKREEEE, SLSSHH, SNAP, SPTAK, SRREE, SSHUK,
SSSWWISSHHH, SVASH, SVBEEP, SZIT, THAKOMPH,
THWAT, TUNGK, TUNK, TWANG, TWANNG, VROOSH,
VWAM, VWAP, WHAZRASH, WHREEEP, WHREEP,
WREEEP, ZAPOW, ZAPT, ZRASH, ZWIP, ZZRAKSH,
ZZRAP, ZZRASH, ZZZOTZH, ZZZRATCH, ZZZT,
ZZZZTHSHYEEK [see Blade, Bullet, Gun, Missile, Mortar]
Whirring / Spinning: WHRRRR, WHRRRRR-TCHAK [see
Mechanical]

Appendix A: Base Forms

Comic book words are noted for extra letters within the base. These letters often have a specific purpose - to indicate magnitude or volume and duration of the sound etc. The opposite, where letters are removed to show an abbreviated or interrupted sound, occurs as well.

A	AWRO	BLA
ACHO	BARF	BLABLA
ACKYAK	BABAM	BLACH
AE	BADABOM	BLADRAM
AEK	BADOM	BLADROM
AG	BADOW	BLAHDABOM
AGH	BAH	BLAM
AGHA	BAHWAH	BLAMBLAM
AGHK	BALOM	BLAMP
AGK	BAM	BLANG
AGOGAH	BAMF	BLAP
AH	BANG	BLASH
AHA	BANGCRASH	BLAST
AHAH	BAOM	BLAT
AHEM	BAOUM	BLATBLAT
AHGH	BAP	BLATCH
AHOHGAH	BAPDEBOW	BLEAH
AHR	BARAROM	BLECH
AIE	BARF	BLEP
AIEGH	BAROM	BLESH
AK	BASH	BLEUGHZ
AKH	BATANG	BLIF
AOG	BAW	BLIKX
AOGAOGAO	BAZAK	BLINK
AR	BDAM	BLINKDIT
ARARGH	BDAMD	BLIP
ARARGLE	BDOK	BLOIT
ARF	BDOW	BLONK
ARG	BDROM	BLOP
ARGH	BELCH	BLORP
ARH	BEOW	BLORSH
ARO	BEP	BLOSH
AROGA	BEYOP	BLUB
AROGAH	BHWOM	BLUNT
ARUF	BIF	BMPH
AW	BING	BOAM
AWK	BINGBONG	BOING

BOINGSMACK	BUDA	CHINK
BOINK	BUDAB	CHINKCHKCH-AK
BOK	BUDABUDA	
BOM	BUDOM	CHINKCNKCH-AK
BOMBOMBOP	BUDURP	
BOMEROM	BUHBOM	CHIP
BOMKABOM	BUL#$%¢&*!	CHOK
BONG	BUMP	CHOKE
BONK	BUR	CHOM
BOP	BURP	CHOMP
BOSH	BURPXK	CHOMPLE
BR	BUZ	CHOMSKH
BRACK	BWAHAHAHA	CHONK
BRAK	BWAK	CHONT
BRAKA	BWAKT	CHOP
BRAKABRAKA-BRAKA	BWAM	CHOW
	BWE	CHPOW
BRAKOM	BWOM	CHRAK
BRAKT	BWOP	CHTHZ
BRAM	BWUMPT	CHUCKLE
BRAOM	BZ	CHUD
BRAOWN	BZAP	CHUF
BRAP	BZAR	CHUGACHUGC-HUGCHUG
BRATATAT	BZCRACK	
BRATCH	BZOR	CHUK
BRAX	BZT	CHUNK
BRDAP	CARAM	CLACK
BRENG	CAWE	CLACKITYCLA-CK
BREP	CHABAM	
BRESH	CHACHUNK	CLANG
BRING	CHAK	CLANK
BRIT	CHAKA	CLAP
BRM	CHAKACHAK	CLAPCLAP
BRNGT	CHAKT	CLICK
BROK	CHAM	CLIK
BROUM	CHAPOWPOW	CLINK
BRAP	CHASH	CLIP
BRP	CHATCHOM	CLONG
BRT	CHCHASH	CLONK
BRZAP	CHEWA	CLOP
BRZT	CHEYEW	CLOPS
BTAM	CHF	CLUNK
BTHWAKT	CHIK	COM
BTOK	CHIKT	CONK
BTOM	CHING	CR

110

CRACK	EYAGH	FOM
CRAK	EYAH	FOMP
CRAKWOM	EYARGH	FOP
CRANK	EYARGX	FOSH
CRASH	EYOW	FP
CREAK	EYUK	FRAK
CREK	FACHOW	FRAP
CRICKCRACK	FAGROLANA	FRAPFT
CROM	FAHBHAM	FROM
CRSHK	FAK	FROSH
CRUMP	FAM	FRUNK
CRUNCH	FAP	FRZAK
CRZPT	FASH	FSH
DANG	FASHOM	FSHOM
DASH	FASHUNK	FSHPLAP
DET	FAWHUMP	FSHST
DING	FAZ	FSIP
DINGALINGA	FEOP	FST
DINGILINGA	FEOT	FT
DINGING	FEP	FTHOM
DINKDINKDINKDINK	FERIP	FTOM
	FERSPLASH	FUD
DIT	FITZROWER	FUHWHOM
DOH	FIZ	FUMP
DOINK	FIZAZIT	FUP
DOM	FLADIP	FWABOK
DON	FLADOING	FWACH
DOT	FLAM	FWACKT
DRING	FLANG	FWAK
DUBDUBDUBDUBDUBDUB	FLAPTAPTAP	FWAKOM
	FLASH	FWAP
DUMTIDUM	FLICK	FWAT
DUNT	FLIK	FWATHOM
DWAT	FLOF	FWE
DWE	FLOFLOFITYFLIFLIFLOFDAFLAF	FWHE
E		FWIBTH
EAGH		FWIP
ECH	FLOIP	FWISK
EHAUGH	FLON	FWISKITYFWASK
EK	FLOP	
EO	FLSH	FWIZACH
EP	FLUMP	FWOM
ERGH	FLUP	FWOP
EUW	FLUTCH	FWOSH
EYA	FOF	FWROSH

FWUD	GLING	HACKGACKIKL-ESHLIK
FWUMP	GLIP	
FWZAM	GLIT	HAH
FZ	GLITCH	HAHA
FZAKL	GLOCHLE	HAHAHAHOHA-HO
FZASH	GLOING	
FZL	GLOMP	HAI
FZOSH	GLONG	HAKGASP
FZRATCH	GLOP	HALPYA
FZS	GLORP	HAR
FZT	GLUB	HAUGH
GA	GLUG	HAUGHM
GACK	GLUGLUG	HAYAH
GADANG	GLUK	HE
GADOING	GLUMP	HEP
GADONG	GLUMPH	HEY
GAG	GLUP	HEYUH
GAGAKTHOF	GLUTCH	HIC
GAGH	GNA	HIS
GAH	GNAR	HIST
GAHAK	GOBLEGOBLE	HIYAH
GAK	GOING	HM
GALON	GONG	HMPH
GAPLORK	GONK	HN
GAR	GORE	HNGN
GARGH	GOTCHA	HNH
GASHKLITZKA	GR	HO
GASHLIKT	GRA	HOHA
GASHLITZGA	GRAH	HONKHONK
GASP	GRAR	HOP
GDONG	GRGUK	HORAY
GEH	GRING	HOT
GENGEN	GROAR	HRN
GEP	GRON	HUK
GEZ	GRONK	HUM
GING	GROWL	HUR
GINGING	GRUNCH	HURG
GINK	GULP	HUYECH
GLABADAP	GURG	HWOKSH
GLAG	GURGLE	HYUK
GLAK	GWAP	IFPFP
GLANGADANG	GWAR	INGALINGALI-NGALINGALIN-GALING
GLAR	GYARH	
GLAWK	GZT	
GLEP	HA	IYIYI

JEZ	KCHOW	KLUNK
K	KCHUNK	KNOCK
KABAM	KEK	KNOK
KABASH	KERASH	KNOKNOCK
KABLOM	KERBASH	KOF
KABOM	KERPLASH	KONK
KACHOM	KERSMASH	KPOW
KACHONK	KERSPLASH	KRACK
KACHUNK	KERUNCH	KRACKLE
KACK	KHAK	KRADABOM
KADOM	KHRASH	KRAGSH
KADONK	KI	KRAK
KAF	KIDO	KRAKADOM
KAFKAF	KIF	KRAKADOM
KAHAK	KIKITIKIKIKITI-	KRAKATOW
KAHIKE	KINGKONG	KRAKC
KAK	KIPUCKATASP-	KRAKCH
KAPF	OP	KRAKL
KAPOK	KITONG	KRAKLE
KAPOKPOK	KLACK	KRAKOM
KAPOW	KLAK	KRAKOW
KAPTHOM	KLAKATAKLA-	KRAM
KARASH	KATA	KRANCH
KARASHBOMB-	KLAKT	KRARASH
AM	KLANG	KRASH
KAROM	KLANGK	KRATAKATAK-
KAROSH	KLANK	ATAKATAM
KARUMP	KLANKT	KRATHAM
KARUNCH	KLASHT	KRATINKLE
KASH	KLICK	KRE
KASPANG	KLIK	KREAK
KATCHOM	KLIKGRON	KREK
KATHRASH	KLIKITAKLKITA	KRESH
KATL	KLIKLAK	KRIK
KATOF	KLIMP	KRISH
KATOM	KLINK	KRITCH
KATOSH	KLINKADINK	KRIZ
KATRANG	KLINKGLINK	KRK
KAW	KLOM	KRNCH
KAWHOM	KLOMP	KROM
KAWHUMP	KLON	KROSH
KAWHUMPH	KLONK	KRUK
KAZAK	KLOP	KRUMP
KBAM	KLUD	KRUNCH
KCHOM	KLUG	

KRUNCHKRINKLEKRINKLEKRITCH	NF	PHT
	NG	PHTOP
	NGH	PHTOW
KRUNTCH	NO	PIKPIKPIK
KSH	NOK	PING
KSHFWOM	NOKNOK	PINGPANG
KTAK	NYAH	PITERPAT
KTAKTAKBALOWM	NYAHAHA	PITOIE
	NYAKGNIFUNK	PIUNG
KTANG	NYARGH	PLAF
KTASH	NYARL	PLASH
KTHUMP	NYRL	PLEP
KTHUNK	O	PLICK
KTOW	OF	PLIK
KUD	OFPH	PLINK
KUG	OH	PLIP
KUHWANG	OMIGOD	PLIPLE
KUK	OPS	PLOBLE
KUMP	ORG	PLOIPLE
KUNK	OSH	PLOK
KURONCH	OUCH	PLOP
KWAM	OUTA	PLOPLE
KWOMP	OW	PLOPLOPLOP
KWONG	OWO	PLORF
KWUF	PADAP	PLORK
KZAK	PAF	PLORP
KZAT	PAF	PLORTCH
LEBOM	PAH	PLOUF
M	PAN	PLOW
MABIT	PANG	PLUNK
MBUHWHAM	PAROM	PLURP
MEOROWGH	PCHOM	POF
MEOROWGSH	PEK	POFT
MF	PEKPEKPEK	POING
MHM	PFHT	POINK
MO	PFT	POIT
MOWM	PHAK	POK
MPH	PHEW	POM
MUNCH	PHFISHT	POMF
MWA	PHFT	POMP
MWUH	PHO	PONG
N	PHOK	POP
NA	PHONT	POPAPOPABOP
NAH	PHROM	POT
NAW	PHSHOSH	POW

PR
PRAYK
PRUKT
PRZAT
PSH
PTAK
PTANG
PTHOM
PTHUMP
PTO
PTOEY
PTOK
PTOM
PTOW
PUFPUF
PUNCH
PWAKAPWOM
PWE
PWOM
QUACKWAKW-
AK
R
RA
RAH
RAKT
RAP
RAPRAPRAP
RAR
RARGH
RATAT
RATATAT
RAUGH
RE
RG
RGL
RHUM
RIBIT
RING
RINKRIK
RIP
RMBL
ROAR
ROARARL
ROARL
ROL

ROR
ROSH
ROWF
ROWR
RUBADUBDUB-
ADUBADUB
RUF
RUM
RUMBLE
RUNCHT
RYENK
RZT
S
SCARF
SCHLICK
SCHLIKT
SCHPLOK
SCHWOK
SCRATCHSCRA-
TCH
SCRE
SCREAM
SCRECH
SCREK
SCRNCH
SFROSH
SH
SHABABOM
SHABLAM
SHADAP
SHAK
SHAKITYSHAK-
ESHAKE
SHAKOM
SHAKOW
SHAKT
SHARAK
SHAZAM
SHAZAP
SHAZATZ
SHAZHIC
SHBLAM
SHCHUK
SHF
SHFOM

SHFOSH
SHIK
SHIKA
SHIKASHIKA
SHING
SHKILITZ
SHKLAP
SHKLIZORTCH
SHKLORT
SHKREUH
SHKSH
SHKSHKT
SHLIP
SHLOMP
SHLOP
SHLORP
SHLURP
SHMAMP
SHOBEDO
SHOBODAHBED-
AH
SHOKASHOKAS-
HOKA
SHOM
SHOP
SHOPOF
SHOSH
SHOW
SHPIKLE
SHPLEP
SHRABOM
SHRACK
SHRAK
SHRAKAKAKA-
KAKAKAKA
SHRAKOM
SHRASH
SHRAZAK
SHRIEK
SHRING
SHROM
SHROZH
SHS
SHSHPRITZ
SHTOM

SHTUP	SKRKRE	SPATZ
SHUK	SKROINCH	SPAZOSH
SHUM	SKRONK	SPING
SHUNK	SKRUK	SPITZ
SHVRAM	SKRUNCH	SPKANG
SHWAK	SKUP	SPLAK
SHWAM	SKWAKO	SPLANG
SHYEK	SKWAPO	SPLASH
SHYMS	SKWEK	SPLASHLE
SHZT	SLAM	SPLAT
SHZTHS	SLAMDUNK	SPLAZATCH
SIZLE	SLANK	SPLAZITCH
SIZLESITZ	SLAP	SPLAZOSH
SKAK	SLAPITYSLAP	SPLITCH
SKAKOM	SLERP	SPLOIT
SKAPOW	SLOK	SPLOP
SKARASH	SLOP	SPLORCH
SKE	SLORPH	SPLORK
SKLANG	SLOTCH	SPLORP
SKLAZONCHO	SLRK	SPLOSH
SKLIK	SLSH	SPLOTCH
SKLOP	SLURP	SPLUBLE
SKLORP	SLURPCRUNCH	SPLUT
SKLORPSKX	SMACK	SPMAMP
SKLOSH	SMAK	SPOF
SKLUTCH	SMASH	SPOPLE
SKOM	SMEK	SPRAKOW
SKOMPH	SNAK	SPRANGWAH
SKR	SNAKT	SPRAY
SKRAKABOM	SNAP	SPRIZITZ
SKRAM	SNF	SPROING
SKRASH	SNIF	SPROING
SKRAW	SNIK	SPRUK
SKRAWK	SNIKT	SPTAK
SKRAZAK	SNORT	SPUTSPUTCHU-
SKRAZH	SNUF	KSPUT
SKRE	SOB	SPWANG
SKRECH	SOCK	SPWAP
SKRE	SOK	SPWE
SKREK	SPABASH	SQUEFROP
SKREKLE	SPAK	SQUIRT
SKREL	SPAKRASH	SQUISH
SKREOW	SPAMAMP	SQULRCH
SKRIKSH	SPANG	SRAK
SKRISH	SPASH	SRE

SREK	THAP	THWOCK
ST	THAPLOF	THWOK
STOK	THCHTH	THWOM
STOM	THITHTHITHTH-ITH	THWOP
STOMPUH		THWOW
STONG	THKAM	THWRAKAPW-OM
SVASH	THLIK	
SVBEP	THLOP	THWUK
SWACK	THLORP	TICK
SWAP	THLUCK	TIK
SWASH	THMP	TING
SWAT	THOIP	TINKLE
SWATHZWHO-UM	THOK	TINKLETINKINK
	THOM	TO
SWIF	THOMP	TOB
SWISH	THONGK	TOC
SWOK	THONK	TOCK
SWOP	THOP	TOK
SWOSH	THP	TOM
SWUMP	THRAKAKAKA-KAKA	TONG
SZH		TONK
SZHK	THRP	TRANGTRANG
SZIK	THRUMP	TRI
SZIT	THRUNCH	TRIUW
SZT	THUBALUPTH-UBALUPTHUB-ALUP	TROMP
TA		TUNGK
TADA		TUNK
TAK	THUD	TWANG
TAKATAKATAK	THUDOM	TWEN
TANG	THUDUD	TWEP
TAP	THUGAWUNK	TWING
TAPTAP	THUK	TZ
TATA	THUMK	TZAPT
TATARATARA-TARA	THUMP	TZING
	THUMPTHUMP	TZNG
TATATATA	THUNK	TZT
TCHAK	THUP	UFT
TCHIKT	THURCH	UGH
TCHOC	THWACK	UGKH
TCHUNK	THWAK	UH
TEHE	THWAM	UHM
THAK	THWASH	UHN
THAKOMPH	THWAT	UHNF
THAKT	THWIP	ULP
THAM	THWIT	UMHM

UMPH	WAMP	WRZ
UN	WAP	WUD
UNG	WE	WUMF
UNGH	WEOWE	WUMP
UNH	WEOWEOWE	WUNK
UNKLIK	WEOWEOWEO	Y
UNPH	WHACK	YA
URF	WHAM	YAFSLISH
URG	WHAMB	YAG
URGH	WHANG	YAGH
URK	WHAP	YAH
URP	WHAZRASH	YAHAGH
URPH	WHE	YAHO
URPTSTFOF	WHIP	YAIE
URUGH	WHIR	YAK
VARHOM	WHIRWHIR	YAYAYAH
VAROM	WHIZ	YAYAYAYAYAH
VAROMROWM	WHO	YECH
VATHROM	WHOM	YEH
VING	WHOMP	YEOUCH
VIP	WHOPE	YEOW
VLURSH	WHOPWHOP	YI
VOM	WHOPWHOPWH-	YIKES
VOMAROMA	OPWHOPWHO	YIPY
VOSH	WHOSH	YOHO
VOWM	WHR	YOW
VRAM	WHREP	YUG
VRE	WHRTCHAK	YUM
VRET	WHUD	Z
VRM	WHUDWHUD	ZACHITY
VROM	WHUK	ZAM
VROMSPOSH	WHUMF	ZANG
VROSH	WHUMP	ZAP
VRUM	WHUNK	ZAPOW
VRZM	WHUTCH	ZAPT
VRZMVRZM	WOK	ZARCH
VS	WOM	ZAT
VSH	WOMO	ZAZIK
VWAM	WOMP	ZCHATHZ
VWAP	WOSH	ZERK
VWAPGARIEPV-ROM	WOUI	ZEZE
	WOWOWO	ZHIP
VZT	WRAKT	ZICH
WA	WREP	ZIK
WAK	WROK	ZIKA

ZIKZIKZIK	ZOTZH	ZTZT
ZING	ZOWIE	ZTZTZ
ZINK	ZPFT	ZURK
ZIP	ZRAK	ZVIPT
ZITZITZIZIZIZ	ZRAKSH	ZVPT
ZIZ	ZRAKT	ZVT
ZIZAK	ZRAP	ZWAK
ZLIKT	ZRARKT	ZWAKT
ZOAM	ZRASH	ZWAZASH
ZOM	ZRATCH	ZWIP
ZONK	ZT	ZWIT
ZOSH	ZTHSHYEK	ZWOSH

Appendix B: Submissions

General Submissions
If you find a word, definition, or earlier citation not included in this dictionary, please send a photocopy of the page it appears upon, as well as of the cover and credit pages, to the KA-BOOM! project for consideration.

Comics Publishers
Send a complete copy of the published comic. If you wish to have specific images considered for inclusion in an illustrated version of KA-BOOM! please send artwork (not originals) and release form with publisher's contact information. Comics and artwork will not be returned.

KA-BOOM! @ Mora Publ.
13226 - 104 Ave., Suite 308
Surrey BC, Canada V3T 1V1

Appendix C: Reference

KA-BOOM! A Dictionary of Comic Book Words is listed in the following works as reference and bibliographic material:

The Complete Idiot's Guide to Cartooning (Paperback) by
Arnold Wagner, Shannon Turlington
ISBN: 0028643798

Jazz Up Your Japanese with Onomatopoeia (Paperback) by
Hiroko Fukuda, Tom Gally (Translator)
ISBN: 477002956X

Printed in the United States
116263LV00002B/223/A